THE MAKING AND THE RE-MAKING OF A CODEPENDENT MIND

A Journey Into and Out
of Codependency

Brian Birdbell
with Stephanie

Birdbell Publishing

To all those who love and have loved us, however imperfectly, and to all of those we imperfectly love.

"*I am constantly defining my selves, for I am, as we all are, made up of so many different parts. But when those selves war within me, I am immobilized, and when they move in harmony, or allowance, I am enriched, made strong.*"

AUDRE LORDE

CONTENTS

PART ONE - THE MAKING OF A CODEPENDENT MIND

CHAPTER 1: CODEPENDENT BEGINNINGS

Codependency is not a disease. I did not catch it or cure it. It was not passed down to me through my genetic inheritance. I was not born with it. It is not a personality trait. I am not codependent like I am introverted, or clever, or conscientious, or adventurous. Rather, codependency is a set of learned behaviors, behaviors that once served me well. Faced with situations in which my needs were not being met or I felt unsafe, I adopted these behaviors as an effective response. I adapted. Human beings have been doing this for hundreds of thousands of years; our ability to adapt to novel situations and environments has been critical to our survival as a species.

When I was young, I received signals from my

environment — my family, my friendships, my community — that the world was unpredictable, chaotic, hostile and sometimes violent. The codependent behaviors allowed me to feel some measure of control in situations where, as a child, I had very little power. The problem with the set of behaviors, clustered together under the heading of codependency, is that outside of that initial environment, they became maladaptive. Meaning, they began to prevent me from finding and creating the kinds of relationships with other people that I desperately needed and desired, ones in which I felt seen, safe and connected.

Not only did they become a barrier to intimate, loving relationships, they got me entangled with disordered people, stuck in toxic friendships and romantic relationships and left me feeling lonely, resentful and depressed for most of my adult life. Although the environment had changed and I was no longer a powerless child, these behaviors had become so habituated, so automatic, they were my default way of relating to others.

Codependent behaviors are interpersonal in nature and form as a result of human interaction. Once conditioned, any or all of the behaviors may occur to some extent during casual interactions with strangers all the way up to enmeshed relationships. When discussing the behaviors that fall under the umbrella of codependency, it's important to note that all of them are normal, natural human reactions to other people. The problem arises when these reactions become pathological — inauthentic and compulsive.

Here are the most common behaviors that are grouped as codependency and what the codependent versions have looked like in my life:

Feeling responsible for others' emotions: I was led to feel that other people's emotional reactions are unsafe, and that I was somehow directly implicated in resolving or managing those emotions.

Compliance: I felt as though other people were more powerful or more important, so would often default to a position of compliance, regardless of what I actually felt or believed.

People pleasing: Because I had an exaggerated fear of disappointing or upsetting other people, I often wound up just telling people what I thought they wanted to hear, or behaving how I thought they wanted me to behave.

Caretaking: I went out of my way to keep the most threatening people in my life safe physically, emotionally, financially, sexually in an attempt to indirectly keep myself safe. This caretaking was often at my own expense or at the expense of others in my life who were less of an immediate threat.

Lack of boundaries: As a result of the overemphasis placed on other people's wants, needs and desires, I ignored my own boundaries and compromised my identity thus putting myself and people around me at risk.

The word codependency is an admittedly misleading one. I came across the term a handful of times but didn't delve deeply into its meaning even when, at one point in my early twenties, my best friend and I wondered if we were codependent. The two of us felt too dependent on each other and unable to cope outside of the bubble of safety we had formed. We didn't realize that what we thought of as codependent wasn't what the term was referring to at all and at that point, I didn't explore it further.

I continued to randomly stumble across the term but it didn't resonate despite my being very much in the throes of codependent behaviors. Years later, while in an abusive romantic relationship, the term came up again in a group therapy session. I can't remember why, but it was suggested I try a CoDA meeting (Co-Dependents Anonymous), which I did. The way I remembered it being presented there was that codependency was more of an addiction in which the codependent person somehow becomes dependent on caring for or even controlling other people, usually other disordered people with addictions of their own, most commonly alcoholism. This wasn't my experience, so once again, I put the idea out of my mind.

Ultimately, I have not found it useful to think of codependency as an addiction. That language suggests that it is the behaviors themselves that are the root of the problem. While it's true that people with codependent behaviors can get stuck in toxic relationships with other disordered people, including people with dependency disorders like alcoholism, the codependent person isn't necessarily there because they are *addicted* to caretaking. Far more likely is that they ended up caring for a disordered person because they had existing codependent habits and behaviors that were activated in that relationship.

More helpful I think is to approach codependent behaviors as learned, strategic, adaptive responses to feelings of powerlessness, to emotional pain. These behaviors function as a *solution* to the pain and/or powerlessness people experience. Unfortunately, the solution is not effective in the long run. Once the behaviors become habitual and disordered, they are maladaptive in that they counterproductively cause more pain and powerlessness than they relieve.

Like most disorders, I think it's helpful to think of codependency as falling on a spectrum of severity. People who find themselves inadvertently stuck for a period of time in a caretaking pattern with a disordered person might fall on the less severe end of this spectrum, if they can even be considered codependent at all. Neither caring for people nor trying to please them is necessarily disordered behavior. It's when these behaviors become compulsive that a person will start to move along towards the more severe end of the spectrum; the behaviors start to significantly compromise their relationships and their own needs and desires. By the time a person gets to the severe end of the codependency spectrum, the behaviors are much more unconscious, automatic and all-encompassing and can result in a loss of identity and autonomy.

I spent most of my life on the severe end of the codependency spectrum. Fortunately what has been learned, can be unlearned. What has been made, can be re-made. In order to do that, however, I needed to go back to the beginning, to the environment in which I learned these behaviors. I needed the origin story.

My Origin Story

My immediate family consisted of myself, two parents and an older brother. My dad worked at an office on the weekdays, while my mom took care of us kids at home. We lived in a comfortably-sized house in a relatively safe, suburban neighborhood, near a big park and all of the schools that I would attend. My parents involved me and my brother in various activities from an early age, like cub scouts, soccer and baseball. We would go camping regularly in our trailer, sometimes going on group outings with a club for families with young children. There were family friends who lived nearby with kids close to our ages that we'd visit and we had fairly regular contact with extended family: grandparents, aunts, uncles. We attended church every Sunday. For the most part, I remember a sense of security and predictability at home.

Neither one of my parents were abusive people. Neither of them had some kind of entitlement or delusions of grandeur. On average, they seemed to get along with each other and the atmosphere in our house when we were together was generally calm. They felt like good people who meant well for themselves, for my brother and me, and for our family.

My parents are both alive, still married, living together and until recently, lived in the same house where I grew up. I wasn't close with my parents or my brother after leaving the house, but we kept in touch and got together regularly for holidays. We maintained a connection with each other that I never quite understood, but somehow felt fine, comfortable. That's basically how I viewed my relationship with my family before doing any of the work I've now done to understand myself.

For years there was something about my childhood,

my family, that I felt I needed to protect; something that kept me from being honest with myself about my experiences. That there didn't seem to be any kind of major conflict between anyone in my family and overall I felt comfortable around them made me want to hold onto certain narratives. I think, like most people, I generally divided my experiences into buckets of *good* and *bad*. For the people I was able to more easily label as *bad* and particularly for those who were no longer in my life, it was easy: *bad* bucket. However, for those that were still in my life, like my family, I just wanted to throw into the *good* bucket and keep that view intact. But experiences are rarely that simple or cut and dry.

While I was able to acknowledge to an extent some of the negative behaviors of my parents, I fell short of looking at how I was affected by their behaviors. It's as if I felt that by thinking of anyone in my family in a bad light, I wasn't being fair and that the universe would somehow judge me harshly for those thoughts. My parents were loving people that provided for me — how dare I think anything bad about them, let alone say it out loud? However it was important for me to learn that having negative experiences with people doesn't necessarily mean they are bad people and that not all bad behavior is abusive. I can still love someone and want them in my life, while also being honest about how that relationship affected me. I came to understand that my incomplete, misleading beliefs and stories about my early experiences, that my always putting my family in the *good* bucket, wasn't helping me; I had to be honest about my full experience. Understanding my family of origin, honestly looking at the impact on me of certain experiences, was the beginning of understanding my own behaviors and was crucial to my self-awareness and healing.

One of the more significant things to have an early impact on me was the way my dad handled his emotions, most notably the way he often defaulted to anger responses. He was an extremely impatient person and seemed to experience significant anxiety when faced with any lack of control of his surroundings. He was very routine-oriented and had a hard time if things didn't go the way he hoped or planned, or if something was more difficult than he had expected. When that happened, whatever the reason, he would get very flustered and lash out in anger. The outbursts were loud and sharp, and usually involved cursing. His tone was very frightening and destabilizing for me, and I still feel the effects to this day when I hear it.

His angry outbursts were directed at anything and everything. Sometimes they were directed at me, sometimes my brother, sometimes my mom, but just as often they were directed at things around him: objects, situations. He would fly off the handle at anything that caused him a sense of frustration or loss of control. Some of the more common ones: when the garage door didn't latch properly; if he discovered ants anywhere in the house; if something wasn't functioning the way he wanted it to; calls from telemarketers. Leaving the house was also often difficult for him since it would involve an increase of elements beyond his control, especially when driving — he lashed out at traffic, at people driving badly, if he was having trouble navigating.

The tone of those angry outbursts frightened me, regardless of who or what they were directed at, although they had an even bigger impact when they were directed at me, my brother or my mom. Sometimes the anger was directed at everyone in the house. If someone left a light on, didn't close a door, didn't put something back in the correct place, or left a wet spot on a countertop, he would shout something that usually included "god dammit," among other things.

Obviously, when I was a young child, there were a lot of things I didn't know how to do or do well. I also didn't always act in the way he expected or wanted me to. Any time this disconnect caused frustration in him, the result was usually that same angry outburst. For example, doing math flashcards with me or helping my brother and me with our monthly boy scout paper drives often resulted in outbursts as he got frustrated perhaps by our lack of understanding or speed.

The anger directed at my mom, brother or me wasn't

always because of something we did "wrong;" sometimes it was just that he had an idea of something one or all of us should do, and if anyone didn't want to do it for whatever reason, he would get angry. Or if he had advice for how to do something and one of us wanted to do it a different way. In those instances he had a common phrase he would include in the resulting angry explosion — "fine, I don't care anymore!" Though obviously he did care and in reality he usually wasn't giving up when he said that.

The majority of the time, my dad was a good-natured, jovial guy, joking around a lot and playing with my brother and me; I feel the effects of those experiences too. In general, I wasn't afraid of my dad or in some kind of a permanent state of fear, but I was definitely afraid of those outbursts of anger and impatience. I found myself trying to figure out how to avoid them however I could, by noticing specific things that set him off and by doing my best to not irritate him. If I failed in those efforts, I would try to find a way to calm him down as quickly as possible. I felt unsafe when he was angry. This need to diffuse my dad's anger and appease him goes back as far as I can remember. I was learning that I couldn't really trust one of my caretakers, that emotions were scary and that I needed to somehow manage my dad's anger. I remember how quickly his emotional switch could flip from anger to something else as long as he was successfully appeased or if he was distracted by something else. Minutes later he could be laughing again as if nothing had happened.

It wasn't just me that needed to avoid or contain my dad's anger, my mom and brother were also in the line of fire. They both used similar tactics as I did — avoid situations and behaviors that would likely cause an explosion and if one happened, attempt to appease, soothe or pacify my dad. I have no memories of my mom sticking up for me when my dad was directing his anger at me, but I do remember times when the anger was directed at her and she tried to fight back; it never seemed to work. My dad would just escalate and she would back down. In that way, my mom modeled compliance behavior as an appropriate response to his anger. From observing her behavior, I learned how to comply. If someone was angry, upset or frustrated, I needed to figure out how to calm that anger — or stop it before it began.

In addition to my dad's anger, a defining feature of my childhood was my mom's negativity. She seemed to feel powerless over pretty much everything in her life and she expressed her resentment about that to us in various ways. She behaved as if she had no say in things in her life — where we lived, what her role was in her relationship with my dad, the types of family activities we did. But she would make sure we were all aware of her bitterness about those things. She would regularly complain about my dad's behaviors to my brother and me, even when we were young children. She was convinced the universe was out to get her/us: "that's just our family's luck" and "this always happens to us" were common refrains when bad things happened.

My mom was my primary caregiver and I recall a feeling of safety that went with that; she would be the one I usually ran to when I got injured and needed comforting. She was very involved when it came to providing experiences for my brother and me — birthdays, holidays, extracurricular activities; she did a lot for us. In general, I don't have memories of her shouting at me or losing her temper. I remember her as a warm and loving mother. Looking back, however, I can also see the ways in which her negativity impeded her ability to provide me with the love and care that I needed. Her disappointments, resentments, bitterness and depression were always close to the surface. These were clearly painful emotions that she struggled to deal with, similar to how my dad struggled with his painful emotions. Whether it was expressing her frustrations and disappointments about our dad, or with her life in general, my brother and I were often enlisted to provide her validation and support in managing her emotions. My caretaking behaviors definitely came in large part from trying to manage my dad's anger, but they also came from feeling responsible for my mom's powerlessness and negativity.

My mom has described me repeatedly over the years,

including recently, as a "difficult baby" who cried a lot and was clingy. While babies can certainly have different temperaments, and indeed, I may have been difficult in some ways, it is also possible that I cried a lot and was clingy because my needs were not being met. I was a second child, coming less than two years after my brother. My mom had two babies to care for, lived away from her family and support system, and had a husband who did not help much with childcare.

From a difficult baby, I became a very compliant child. This was my version of people pleasing. Some children might become the family clown, or the family mediator, or the golden child — the one who excels at everything. Me — I ate food I didn't like; played sports I didn't enjoy; took piano lessons for years, never complaining that I didn't like playing the piano. It became hard for me to really recognize what I actually wanted, to become my true self. I found myself having difficulty making basic decisions or taking any sort of initiative without deferring to someone else. Not only was I not being true to myself with these behaviors, I was being dishonest with others. I was developing a habit of reflexive dishonesty, betraying myself and not really authentically connecting with other people.

These are not behaviors one is born with. All infants are very comfortable expressing their dislikes, their preferences, their discomfort, their distress. They have to be; that is the only way they can get their needs met. Meeting a child's needs doesn't just mean addressing their physical needs, there are emotional needs as well. Children need love, care and attention. These needs are equally as compelling and important as their physical needs and they regularly make bids to get those needs met. Sometimes those bids can be relentless and aren't always easy to understand or respond to. But what happens when certain types of needs — physical or emotional — are regularly dismissed or reacted to negatively? An example: when my dad used to watch evening news between the time he got home from work and dinner, if any of us made any sort of bid for attention during those times, he would get very upset, waving us away and shouting something like "shhh, listen! I'm trying to listen!" He was telling us, in a forceful, threatening way, that connecting with me, with us, was less important than watching television. Such experiences led me to feel unsafe in expressing my need for his attention, assistance or affection.

All of these experiences played a role in the way I responded to the world around me internally and interpersonally. While I generally felt physically safe and the world around me seemed stable and secure, emotionally and interpersonally, things were much more fraught. Sometimes I would get a playful, engaged father, sometimes an angry, scary father. Sometimes I would get a loving and responsive mother, sometimes a depressed and resigned mother. I unconsciously internalized their emotions as if they were my responsibility. This was the environment that gave rise to my codependent behaviors. From a place of powerlessness, I was learning to put other people's needs ahead of my own; to take them on and feel responsible for them. My needs were not only unimportant, they were often dismissed or overruled. I learned that it was unsafe to upset my dad or disappoint my mother. Far safer was to suppress or ignore my own desires and fall in line with whatever I thought they wanted or needed from me.

My parents worked with what they had. I believed and still believe that they meant well for my brother and me and they both made quite a bit of effort to care for us, within their limitations. I don't carry resentment towards them for the negative experiences, at least not anymore. But to understand how my codependent mind was formed, I had to acknowledge the negative experiences while also acknowledging the positive and recognize that both can be present in the same relationship. I also needed to understand that it was within my home environment that my codependent behaviors started forming; behaviors that I would carry with me into the world outside my house.

CHAPTER 2: TRAUMA

When I started making all of the connections that have led to where I am now, I didn't know very much about trauma. I had heard about Post-Traumatic Stress Disorder (PTSD), but mostly in the context of soldiers returning from war zones, or individuals working in law enforcement or as first responders. I thought of PTSD as something that happened to people who had witnessed or been a part of terrible events; I didn't imagine that it could apply to me. I certainly had unpleasant experiences and been subjected to scary and confusing situations and relationships, but surely those didn't count.

However, as I learned more about trauma through reading and listening to clinicians and scholars, I came to understand that trauma is not *what* happens to you but rather the *effect* it has on you. Trauma is not found in the cut and dry details of the episode, rather it resides in the physical, psychic or emotional damage that is done. Two people can experience the same event and one person can be traumatized while another can escape trauma-free. Think for instance of a bomb exploding with two people standing nearby. It is possible that one person is hit by shrapnel and grievously wounded while the other, by luck, or circumstance, is physically unscathed. Moreover, while that is an example of physical trauma, trauma need not be physical. Emotional wounds and psychic wounds can be as damaging and life-altering as physical ones. Especially as they are often more difficult to recognize, for ourselves and the people around us.

I learned that trauma is not necessarily delivered by way of a singular, dramatic event like a sexual assault, a serious car accident or watching fellow soldiers be killed. These are all terrible events to go through that I imagine could shatter one's sense of safety, compromise one's sense of self and complicate one's relationship to the world. But trauma can also be delivered in dribs and drabs, with such little fanfare that it goes relatively unnoticed and unrecognized. This is referred to as chronic or complex trauma. Examples would be emotional or verbal abuse, or when a person — especially a child — is repeatedly made to feel unsafe or repeatedly gets messages that they are unworthy or defective.

Although many of my family childhood experiences might be considered as less obvious, drawn-out trauma and subjectively less severe, they never-the-less had a traumatic effect on me. My codependent behaviors were responses to the emotional and psychological conditions of my early life. To understand how my codependent behaviors formed is to understand the trauma I experienced in that environment.

New Layers Of Trauma

The trauma I experienced within my family relationships conditioned me to respond codependently, which in turn made me vulnerable to further trauma as I ventured outside my family and my home. An early traumatic relationship I had was a friendship with a boy I'll call G; one that started when I was four and lasted until I was around 10. My experiences with him were especially severe and occurred at such a critical time in my development that I find it helpful to go into some detail as I expand on the idea of trauma and what it does to a person's whole system.

I met G in kindergarten. We met while playing with toys in the classroom and became friends. There were two other kids we were friends with, P and H who I really liked a lot and have fond memories of. I don't actually recall much in the way of negative behaviors from G in the first two years of our friendship, maybe P and H acted as buffers. I do have a vague memory of the way G treated other kids in our class, behavior that goes along with what I came to know about who G was — a bully. Although I don't recall specific behavior directed at me, by second grade, H having already moved away, I remember feeling a wave of fear when P told us he was moving too. His leaving meant it would just be G and me.

G and I were in separate classrooms at that point but we hung out during lunch, we traveled to and from school together, we hung out after school, and we were in Cub Scouts together. We considered ourselves best friends and he was quick to say that to anyone and everyone. He made it clear early on that he didn't want me to hang out with anyone else or try to bring other kids into our circle. G had a lot of access to me, and second grade was when things really started to become difficult with him.

G was verbally and physically abusive towards me. There were various things I'd do that set him off: contradicting him, making him feel embarrassed in some way, saying things he didn't like or in a way he didn't like. He would shout at me or call me names, sometimes punching me in the arms or back. One time he beat me up, knocking me on the ground and repeatedly kicking me all over, mostly in the ribs. I was in constant fear of him, always working to figure out what triggered his attacks and then doing everything I could to prevent them.

In spite of my fear of G, I continued to hang out with him. My ability to respond to threats from other people had been warped by experiences within my family. The way I responded to external threats was not effective in keeping me safe from G; it was keeping me stuck in that friendship.

Threat Responses

Across the animal kingdom, all species including ours, are equipped with automatic responses to environmental threats. The most well known of these are *fight and flight*. For example, if you have a cat or other domestic pet, you might see these two responses almost every day. When a cat sees a dog that it considers a threat, it might prepare to fight by hissing and acting aggressively or it might run and hide under the couch. Whether the cat chooses to fight or flee will depend on its evaluation of the size of the threat and its own temperament and life history.

Somewhat less well-known threat responses, but equally as common, are *freeze and fawn;* responses most commonly used by small animals when confronted with bigger animals. A mouse, for example, is certainly in no position to use the fight or flight response when confronted with a bigger animal. More often than not the mouse will adopt the *freeze* response: stopping in their tracks and becoming very still. This is their way of minimizing their appeal to the threatening animal; perhaps it won't see it or will dismiss the mouse as unimportant and pass it by.

The *fawn* response to threat is also observable particularly to those of us who own dogs. For instance, what does a dog do when threatened or when it perceives anger from their owner? It adopts fawning behavior — tucking its tail between its legs, bowing its head, flattening its ears. Once the dog senses the owner may no longer be angry, it might put its head on the owner's legs and look at them with an expression of deference and appeasement. Dogs are so practiced at fawning that we can be convinced they know what they did was wrong and have learned their lesson. The dog is using the *fawning* response to neutralize a threatening situation.

As a small child, my options for responding to threats were limited. I didn't have the opportunity or the capacity to flee or to fight. I was left with only freeze and fawn when responding to any actions by my parents that I perceived as threatening. Once I met G, and started to experience similar, although much more extreme behaviors, I responded in the same way as with my parents. When he was actively attacking me, I would freeze. That response was usually somewhat effective in that the abuse would temporarily subside. He would stop hitting or insulting me and things would become relatively calm until the next episode, the threat only temporarily neutralized. Knowing there would be other episodes, I used and further developed the fawn behaviors I learned when dealing with my mom and dad. I developed strategies to avoid the next round of abuse, by lining myself up with him as best as I possibly could.

The lessons that I learned at home — that I needed to deny my own wants, needs and desires in exchange for care, attention or safety — were being violently reinforced by G on a daily basis. Thinking of and responding to the needs, wants and attitudes of others was becoming even more deeply ingrained; it was becoming my habitual way of reacting to perceived or real threats. My feelings didn't matter. What I wanted didn't matter. How I thought didn't matter. All that mattered was that I did everything I could to avoid upsetting or disappointing people. If G was happy, I pretended to be happy. If he was sad, I did the same. I mirrored him in every way that I could. We didn't exactly like to do the same things, but I just went along with whatever he wanted to do.

Emotional Trauma

G didn't only abuse me; he was a bully. Although I don't recall seeing him ever physically assault any other kid, he freely used psychological and emotional torment that was unpredictable, frightening and chaotic. In retrospect, I believe he had a complete lack of empathy for others, and that his behavior bordered on sociopathic.

A couple of examples:

A boy that lived across the street from G was in our same carpool. Every day, G spent the drive tormenting him — calling him smelly, mocking and insulting him. One day when this boy saw G and me outside, he brought over his new GI Joe vehicle to show us; it was a troop carrier full of figures. G grabbed it out of his hands, threw it on the ground, smashing it and breaking several of the figures. While all this was happening I remember feeling an overwhelming sense of what I now understand to be empathy for the other kid while also feeling completely helpless to do anything other than stand and watch. After he broke the toy, G turned around and started walking back to his house. I quickly snuck a look at the boy and whispered very quietly, "I'm sorry," before following G; it was all I felt safe doing.

There was a girl who mailed G a letter telling him that she had a crush on him; I was there when he opened the letter. He laughed uncontrollably, then wrote her back telling her he would never go out with her, telling her how ugly she was, writing more cruel, hurtful things. He walked to her house and hand-delivered the letter, while I tagged along and watched. I felt so sorry for her as I stood by powerlessly, knowing how mean the letter was. The next day I saw her crying at school and although I knew why and felt badly for her, I was afraid to express any sympathy to her.

G tormented anyone and everyone and I stood by while he did. I always wondered what I looked like to all of those kids — that quiet boy standing slightly behind pretending to support him, sometimes even fake-laughing when all I really wanted to do was cry. I did nothing to help them; I just stood there, not participating but not acting on their behalf either. So many times I wanted to let the other kids know how sorry I was, to stand *with* them instead of appearing to stand with G, but I couldn't. From those years of experiences with G there grew a huge burden of shame, a feeling I didn't understand and didn't know how to handle.

Along with the outward behaviors that I was developing to keep myself physically safe — people pleasing and compliance — I was also learning ways of keeping myself safe emotionally. The fear and shame I consistently felt at home and with G were too confusing and painful for me to process. So I started developing ways of avoiding or burying my emotions altogether. I would tell myself stories to defuse the painful memories and turn them into something I could handle. Or I buried them deep in some small compartment in my mind, never looking at them consciously again.

My childhood was a very solitary, lonely one. It felt as if I couldn't rely on anyone else to keep me safe; I just had to do my best on my own. My parents didn't ask me how I was feeling or what experiences I was having, and I didn't offer that information to them. I had no idea how to reach out to people for help. My inner life was increasingly chaotic, full of anxiety, fear, shame, sadness and confusion. I felt scared and weak. Once, a classmate witnessed G beating me up and asked me why I hung out with him. My response was just "I don't know." It didn't occur to me that there might be options other than putting all of my effort into just surviving.

G's family moved away when we were in grade five. When he told me they were moving, I remember tearing up. He probably assumed I was sad that he was leaving, but they were tears of relief. I was free of G's daily abuse, but it was out of just pure luck. There was nothing I did to make this happen — no agency on my part, no overcoming of fear or shame. There was nothing my parents did to step in and help, or any other adults for that matter. While I was free of G's particular abuse, I learned absolutely nothing from the experience that would help me heal or start to form healthier behaviors and emotional connections. The damage was done, and from then on, everyone I came in contact with was just another potential G, as far as my body and subconscious was concerned.

Emotional Avoidance

The world is often a confusing, complex and hostile place. The more information we have, the better we are able to navigate it successfully. Our emotions give us a great deal of information about the world. They have been finely attuned by millions of years of evolution to give us 'actionable intelligence' about our environment. Fear — flee! Love — stay! Anger — fight! Guilt — stop! Given the opportunity to develop and mature, our emotions can be reliable guides, walking with us as we move through our lives, directing us towards opportunities and away from threats.

I wasn't just afraid of other peoples' emotions, I was afraid of my own. Instead of being reliable guides, my emotions were a source of confusion and anxiety. I didn't trust myself or my ability to act on them, so I did everything I could to avoid them. Healthy emotional processing wasn't modeled to me by anyone close to me, including my parents, and I never felt safe enough to reach out to anyone for help. So I went it alone, figuring out the best ways I could to protect myself from my emotions, instead of learning from or resolving them.

I became very practiced at dissociation and compartmentalization. They became my default responses to my emotional pain. I would sense that something — a thought, an experience, an interaction with someone — was making me feel a certain way and if that feeling was one that I had previously identified as painful, I set that feeling aside, ignored it and distracted myself. If those feelings came up during something volatile, like when I was in the middle of being attacked by G, I just froze and dissociated, disconnected myself from any emotions. Once the attack was over, the compartmentalization would take over and bury the fear and shame that I had just experienced somewhere deep within me.

Like so many strategies that I employed, compartmentalization is not always bad in every situation. Sometimes we have to set aside certain feelings in order to take some kind of action for our own safety or the safety of others. We can think of first responders, for example, who need to set aside their fears and emotions in order to rush into a burning building or take care of a wounded patient. I was not compartmentalizing in extreme situations, however, I was doing it habitually, compulsively, whenever a painful emotion threatened to surface. And I would never go back and try to process those emotions. I wasn't resolving anything. The painful emotions became trapped inside of me unprocessed and unhealed. They would just get added to layers of previously unprocessed emotions. Over the years, these layers of emotions continued to build up. The word compartmentalization makes it sounds like everything is neat and ordered, tidily tucked away in boxes. In reality, my inner life was just a big, confusing mess. I had no idea what was really in there and the longer this went on the more difficult it became to even begin to figure it out.

Dissociation and compartmentalization may have

provided immediate relief in emotionally painful situations but in the long term, caused problems. The painful, unprocessed emotions continued to linger as vague feelings of depression and anxiety. I wasn't aware that there were medical diagnoses for those feelings when I was younger, but even once I was aware and was diagnosed with severe depression later in life, it didn't really make a difference. Medication didn't really make a difference. For me, those depressed and anxious feelings were signs from my emotional system that I had unprocessed emotions, ones that were dangerous for my well being. The longer I went on like this, the lower I felt and the more difficult it became to function in society. I wound up being close to or at my full emotional capacity on pretty much an ongoing basis, unable to handle much else. All of this led to extreme feelings of isolation and set me up for additional dysfunctional relationships.

CHAPTER 3: HUMAN CONNECTION

All humans crave connection, it's who we are as a species. Behavior disorders like codependency can make it difficult to form those connections. The codependent behaviors kept me safe by hiding my true self from other people. Eventually I was hiding from myself as well. There was no way to connect with others when I was so disconnected, so fragmented.

By the time my childhood friend G had exited my life in fifth grade, I had a fairly complex system of false signals and misguided reactions that were not setting me up for interpersonal success. From my parents, I learned that other people's needs and emotional responses were not only more important than mine, but that they were my responsibility to manage. Other people's emotions were unpredictable and sometimes chaotic and frightening. During my friendship with G, my codependent habits deepened. Having needs, desires, even feelings of my own felt off-limits, even dangerous. My body became accustomed to being on constant threat alert and I was not prepared for what it would take to form healthy relationships going forward.

While other children were learning who they were as individuals — discovering sources of personal power, learning about their emotions, figuring out how to navigate the complicated world of interpersonal relationships — I was doing none of that. Instead of learning about myself, I was focused on learning about other people so I could manage their emotions and behaviors. Instead of figuring out my wants, needs and desires and how to achieve them, I was becoming very adept at figuring out what other people wanted, needed or desired and how to deliver on those. I was in a suspended state of unhealed trauma and emotional immaturity, with growing layers of shame, fear and resentment.

A new source of shame that came about for me not too long after G moved away was sexual shame, which quickly became severe. Suddenly, it seemed as though everyone was talking about sex, particularly the boys I was around in school and in Boy Scouts. I had no idea what they were talking about or how to find out. I was starting to get very clear messages from those around me about what it meant to be a boy or a man — how to behave and not behave. As far as I could tell, I wasn't living up to any of those expectations.

The layers of shame I was carrying, especially the sexual shame, added to my sense of isolation. I was in constant fear of being exposed for my ignorance and lack of life experience. I didn't see myself as worthy of being part of the social interactions that were going on around me. But as separate as I felt, I still desperately wanted, needed, to belong; but where, and with whom? I had to fit in but I couldn't manage to figure out how. Everyone else seemed to know who they were and how and where they fit, but I had no clue. Overall, my social landscape was one of extreme powerlessness and anxiety. I mostly kept myself small and inconsequential, in hopes of avoiding being a target.

My powerless approach to social interactions combined with the ways I felt about myself led me to passively just accept whoever came along and chose me. As a result and not surprisingly, I usually wound up becoming involved with others who also struggled with their self image or who were socially or emotionally dysfunctional.

Codependency And Other Behavior Disorders

Emotionally mature people interested in authentic

relationships aren't looking for someone who agrees with everything they say. They don't need or even want people who go out of their way to defuse their painful emotions or try to match everything they do. In other words, they don't need or want the kind of skills I developed as a child and young adult; skills I needed to make me feel safe. Unfortunately there are plenty of people out there who are looking to others for compliance and deference; who need it — who demand it. Those were the types of people I mostly became involved with and sadly, these relationships often devolved into abusive relationships.

However, before I get into my relationships with abusive disordered people, I think it would be helpful to explain how things worked with a person from my past who was not abusive, but who was still very much a disordered person. In some ways he was similar to me, but in many ways different. This was my friend E. He and I were best friends for about twelve years, from late high school to well beyond college and it was, up to that time and for a fairly long time afterwards, the closest thing to a safe, connected, intimate relationship that I had. In fact, to this day, it is still the longest relationship I've been in, not counting my family.

E and I had very similar upbringings and similar traumatic experiences. Both of us struggled to understand and express our emotions and both of us found ourselves behaving in ways that we developed to cope with our unhealed traumas; these behaviors doing less and less through the years to actually help us cope. We'd talk for hours mostly about the world around us, offering our interpretations of it although only occasionally hinting at our emotional experiences.

Despite our connection and our many talks about life, ourselves and the world, neither of us managed to gain the emotional awareness we needed to understand what was holding us back. Every year it became more and more difficult for each of us to relate to anyone outside of the safety of our two-person bubble. We increasingly leaned on each other and co-isolated. We would have regular conversations about our desire to find romantic partners, but always fell short of putting in the effort to make that happen. I had too much shame and fear, especially when it came to my lack of sexual experience, so the romantic realm felt off limits to me, almost impossible. We each struggled with depression and would go through periods of heavy alcohol use.

E started to struggle pretty severely emotionally. I did as well, but I was better at compartmentalizing and avoiding all of the emotional signals I was getting — so I kept myself mostly numb. E's emotional challenges, however, intensified as time went on. Rather than trying to actually help him, though, I went to work with my codependent responses and tried to regulate E's emotions. If he was unsatisfied with something, I'd go out of my way to curate his experience; if he was uncomfortable with his surroundings, I'd go out of my way to alter them. E's distress scared me. I needed him to feel safe, because his sense of safety was crucial to mine.

The more he seemed to need it, the more I took on a caretaking role. Even though he wasn't demanding that I do so, I regularly denied my own wants, needs and desires to support him in any way I could. He wanted to play music for a living, and I went to work trying to figure out how to make that happen, spending hours everyday researching the music industry and spending thousands of dollars setting up a studio. I even convinced myself that I wanted the same dream. When he struggled financially, I responded by combining our finances and assuring him it was all fine, it was for the greater good and everything would work out someday. When he found himself needing to escape using tools like alcohol, I not only enabled it, I joined in.

In spite of all those efforts to help, I wasn't necessarily being empathetic. Actually, my caretaking involved very little care. If E expressed dissatisfaction or worry about his situation or his future, I was quick to dismiss his feelings with a "it'll be okay, don't worry" comment. I would deny him the reality of his feelings because I was in denial. Deep down I knew our situation wasn't good, but I was afraid; I didn't want to lose the only safe person I had ever met by trying something different. Eventually things got too difficult for E and he needed more help than I could give — he needed professional help. As a result, we had to go our separate ways.

I regret how hard things got for him and how little what I did actually helped. In fact, I sometimes feel that my efforts actually had the opposite effect. Because at the same time E was struggling, I was also trying to figure out what was wrong with me: Why am I depressed? Why am I anxious? Why am I socially awkward? And so my own confusion and my codependent and somewhat self-centered behaviors — behaviors I thought were driven by my desire to help E but to a degree reflected my knee-jerk need to protect myself — might have, and probably did, make things worse.

What I don't regret from the years of friendship with E was that I had what I still describe as an intimate relationship during a very difficult period of my life. That relationship planted within me a seed of the value, worth and importance of intimate, supportive connections. Even though it was challenging for me in the years to come to access the memory of that aspect of my relationship with E, the muscle memory of that connection got lodged in my subconscious and would come in handy eventually.

Relationships With Narcissists

One of my earliest discoveries around the time I realized I was codependent was that the most damaging relationships I've experienced were with narcissistic people. Consequently, I've done quite a bit reading and researching into narcissism and its connection to codependency. Looking back, I realize I had multiple friendships during my childhood and early adulthood with people whose behaviors were narcissistic. My first two romantic relationships were with women who were extremely narcissistic. I have done extensive reflection on the types of behaviors those friends and romantic partners had, the ways in which they were almost identical to each other, the ways in which they differed, the ways in which I was affected, and how my behaviors looked during those relationships.

Relationships between people with codependent behaviors and people with narcissistic behaviors are especially problematic. Not only did narcissistic behaviors activate my codependent behaviors in the most severe way, my relationships with narcissistic people led to new layers of shame and trauma and brought me dangerously close to ending my life. For that reason, I feel the need to spend some time laying out what I've found to be the most common narcissistic behaviors and how those behaviors interact with codependent behaviors.

The Codependency And Narcissism Connection

Codependency and narcissism, like many behavioral disorders, are most commonly a response to trauma. They are strategies for survival — coping mechanisms to deal with the trauma and to attempt to achieve some level of safety in threatening situations. Two people can have very similar experiences, but develop completely different ways of coping with the resulting trauma.

As it is with codependency, narcissism is a spectrum. Additionally, not all of the behaviors that are described as codependent or narcissistic are exclusive to people described as codependent or narcissistic. Anyone can exhibit codependent and/or narcissistic behaviors from time to time; I know that some of my behaviors over the years could be considered more narcissistic than codependent. It's useful, though, to think about what's driving those behaviors and how, in general, they can be clustered together. When people behave more one way than the other, we would call them a codependent person or a narcissistic person.

Given that both can have roots in childhood trauma, it is not surprising that in some ways, codependency and narcissism are similar. Despite how it may look from the outside, powerlessness and low self-esteem are very much at the center of both a narcissistic and codependent person's experience. Narcissistic people and codependent people have difficulty interpreting, managing and expressing their emotions. Both sets of behaviors can block empathetic responses and so make authentic human connection difficult. There is often a high level of self-centeredness that comes with narcissism and codependency, as much as it may look on the surface as though codependent people are more focused on other people.

In many ways, however, the behaviors that make up codependency and narcissism are effectively polar opposites. One way to understand that opposition is to see it as opposing reactions to the threats of childhood. When under threat, by abuse, neglect, chaos, confusion, one response is to make yourself as small as possible, invisible, and align yourself with the most powerful actors around you (freeze and fawn); another response is to make yourself as large as possible, invincible, and to attack or discard anyone who challenges you (fight and flight). The former is a path to codependency, the latter to narcissism.

For the codependent person, the path to feeling secure is to try to make others feel comfortable at all costs — compliance, people pleasing, caretaking. Codependency is about putting other people's needs first with the hope that if other people feel safe and comfortable, so, by extension, will the codependent person. Narcissistic people take the opposite approach; they make it everyone else's responsibility to make them feel safe and comfortable. The cornerstones of narcissism — grandiosity, entitlement, lack of accountability — are about forcing their needs on everyone else.

Grandiosity, Entitlement And Lack Of Accountability

While codependent people often have a deflated sense of self, quick to see themselves as defective or undeserving, narcissistic people have an inflated sense of self, a grandiosity. I've observed this grandiosity in every person I've known with narcissistic behaviors. They all spent enormous amounts of time crafting an image that provided them with the highest level of validation, support, admiration, praise or envy. Experiences, tastes, hobbies, job performance were always expressed in a grandiose way. Common refrains were that they were the first to do something or to say something in a particular way, or that they were the number one fan of a musical group, or author, or activity. Then, to reinforce their superiority, there was always a hefty dose of dismissal, condescension, or belittlement of other people's tastes. Comments like "you're not a real fan" or "you just started liking that because I did" or "you have boring taste" are examples that were regularly directed *at* me, or were expressed *to* me about others, including people the narcissists considered friends.

As confident as the narcissistic person may appear, though, they are actually quite fragile. Every narcissistic person I've known was engaged in a seemingly never-ending search for people to validate them. When a person was found, the narcissistic person pulled them in and kept them close by whatever methods worked and went out to look for more. Anyone who didn't validate their vision of themselves was avoided, discarded or scorned. Alongside this need for validation was a deep-seated paranoia. They were on constant threat alert and it was extremely destabilizing for them when they encountered people who didn't support the image they created of themselves. I remember well the sheer confusion that came when one of them didn't get the validation they expected, especially if the other person got too close to the truth and called them out on something. The immediate assumption was that there was something very wrong with the *other* person. That was the only acceptable conclusion.

This inflated sense of importance and the need to feel special in turn fuels a deep sense of entitlement. Unlike myself who struggled to feel entitled to even my own needs and desires, my narcissistic friends and partners felt entitled to just about everything. When they wanted something, they felt they deserved it and were owed it. When they perceived it as available, they would demand it. Their needs and desires were to be prioritized at all times. They expected preferential treatment from others, whether from close friends or complete strangers. They also felt entitled to other people, including me — my time, my money, my emotional space, my thoughts, my body and sexuality were all to be available to them.

Another core feature of narcissism is a lack of accountability. Similar to how I would struggle to maintain empathy when in threat response mode, the narcissists in my life would often display a lack of empathy as well, especially when it involved how their own behaviors affected others. When they behaved in such a way that upset other people, they were quick to dismiss those people's concerns and rationalize their actions. If ever I challenged their behavior, they would often run through what I have since learned is a common narcissistic script, represented by the acronym DARVO. They would deny (D) the behavior — "I was just joking" or "I never said/did that." They would attack (A) — "You have no sense of humor" or "You're just stupid/ weak/a loser." And finally they'd reverse the victim and offender (RVO) roles and decide that *they* were the ones being mistreated — "You never listen to me" or "You're lying/you tricked me" or "I'm sick/ tired/hungry and you provoked me".

As a person who was conditioned to respond with codependent behaviors, I was a perfect match for narcissistic people, as a friend or romantic partner. Right from the start, I was prepared to validate and support their vision of themselves. My excessive agreeableness was exactly what they were looking for. They felt entitled to have their needs and wants prioritized and I was used to catering to the needs of other people to the detriment of my own. My goal was to make everyone around me feel safe by taking responsibility for their emotions and experiences, and narcissistic people not only need this, they expect it and demand it. If those demands and expectations were extreme or even threatening, as they often were, my compulsion to continue to provide these things was even greater because I was conditioned to always respond to the biggest threat. And since narcissists are never wrong, I was there to help excuse their behavior, even when it involved abuse of others, or even myself.

Control

Everyone needs to feel as though they have some level of control over their lives. Achieving that feeling can be difficult for many people, especially those who struggle with emotional dysregulation or interpersonal disorders like codependency or narcissism. It can be frightening to feel as though we don't have control over our lives and each individual's response to that fear is going to be different. Both of my parents struggled with their feelings of not being in control in different ways.

My dad's response was more aggressive, controlling others by angry outbursts that elicited fearful compliance. My mom was much more passive, giving in to powerlessness and victimhood thus enlisting other people's sympathy or validation. When a person becomes fixated on trying to change other people to their benefit, either passively or aggressively, things especially start to go awry and we might call that person *controlling*.

Codependent control is usually directed at managing other people's emotions. Because my parents' anger or distress, G's anger or distress, was scary and threatening to me, I developed certain behaviors that could be called controlling or manipulative; behaviors such as lying, pretending to align myself with someone else's feelings, changing my behavior to mirror the behavior of another, dismissing or diminishing other people's painful emotions. However there's also a passivity to such codependent control. For me, it wasn't about trying to change other people, but about trying to make them feel safe and that they had an unconditional ally in me.

Narcissistic control is much more aggressive. For narcissists, feeling safe is about acting on their feelings of entitlement to use people in every possible way. Narcissistic control is about demanding: demanding other's time and energy, demanding compliance, demanding that people not only treat them the way they feel entitled to be treated, but that they be who they need them to be. Narcissists will also lie whenever they need to, in order to keep themselves in control of any situation or to avoid any responsibility.

Codependent and narcissistic control are both at the more severe end of the spectrum of controlling behaviors, but they're quite different in their overall effects on other people. Here's another way to contrast the motivations of codependency versus narcissism when thinking about controlling behaviors. Codependency is more about the need to fit with others to keep yourself safe. Codependent control is about trying to lead others to believe you're achieving that. Narcissism is about the need for others to fit with you. Narcissistic control is about trying to force others to do so.

When these two manipulative personality types come together, it might seem their controlling behaviors mesh or counterbalance each other. However, this type of *balance* can't lead to an authentic, connected relationship that is healthy or empowering because its foundation is toxic at the very core.

CHAPTER 4: TOXIC RELATIONSHIPS

When it comes to defending the narratives they've built about themselves, narcissists will often resort to extreme measures. This is such a common feature of narcissism, that there's actually a term for it — narcissistic abuse. The abuse takes on many forms — emotional, psychological, physical, financial, sexual — and is pervasive in their day to day interactions. However, there are more acute abusive/controlling behaviors that go beyond the everyday when they feel a need to lash out in order to maintain or reassert control. These behaviors include verbal abuse like condescension, belittling, insulting, coercion; volatile rage like shouting or throwing things; contempt or constant criticism; physical violence; and manipulative behaviors like gaslighting or stonewalling.

I experienced some of these abusive behaviors in my friendships with narcissists and I certainly experienced most of them in my first two romantic relationships. I was late to the romance game, but when I joined, I wound up in two back-to-back relationships spanning 12 years with abusive, narcissistic women; first R and then J.

Both of those relationships started in a way that is apparently a page right out of the narcissism playbook — love bombing. Love bombing is when a person is subjected to a destabilizing bombardment of attention from a potential romantic partner or friend, often in the form of constant and relentless communication. It can include being showered with compliments, care, gifts — whatever has the biggest impact.

Relationship Beginnings

R and J's love bombing was extremely disorienting, and I had almost no defenses against it. Both times, I was emerging from long periods of feeling the worst I have ever felt about myself, especially socially and sexually. Both times I was struggling with a great deal of shame about my romantic life. The over-the-top compliments and the sexually suggestive, sometimes explicit, comments seemed to offer up an opportunity to be something other than the sexless, undesirable loser I was scared that I was.

In addition to the love bombing, both R and J started immediately talking and acting like we were already in a relationship. From the earliest conversations, they referenced our shared future and began laying out their expectations of me as a romantic partner. Being chosen was difficult for me to resist. I was used to approaching social interactions with a lack of agency, just accepting whatever came along. When someone chose me, it let me off the vulnerability hook. I didn't have to do any work that might involve rejection. Additionally, I didn't feel I had the right to refuse a relationship if someone was insisting on one with me.

It was easy for me to overlook the confusion that comes with love bombing, since I was already used to not looking at life from a big picture perspective. Life was just a series of moments that made me feel bad or good, and my goal was to chase the good and avoid the bad. There was an excitement and a relief in being chosen so I was quick to mirror their love bombing behaviors. It didn't matter if I had the time, or if I was in the middle of something, I felt the need to respond immediately to every communication. In doing so, I was responding to their entitlement with compliance. This compliance may have emboldened them, because alongside the love bombing, the abusive, controlling behavior began.

R figured out that I hadn't had sex before and teased me heavily for it — confirming what was one of my biggest fears at that point, that my sexual inexperience was shameful. Her teasing was condescending and insulting, but at the same time, she suggested that she was going to relieve that shame by having sex with me. It was like dangling a carrot in front of a rabbit to get it to run faster. Humiliating, but also somehow motivating. Tapping into my sexual shame was extremely effective, but she didn't stop there. Mixed in with her expressions of grandiosity was her utter disapproval, even disdain for almost everything about me — my history, the way I dressed and carried myself, any opinions I expressed, how I behaved socially. She was sure to still include some kind of offset to those comments, like saying how she would go shopping with me to clean up my wardrobe or take me to social events. She was letting me know I was an unattractive loser who should never expect a woman to be interested in me — but she was going to give me a chance. Any resistance on my part was met with more scorn, derision and insults.

Fast forward eight years to when R and I had decided to divorce but were still living together. This is when I met J. Not really met — she reached out to me over social media. In that first conversation, before we even met in person, J asked me to denounce R, to swear to her that there was no way the relationship would be rekindled. She created a similar dynamic as R, implying I was a loser for the way I was handling the divorce, and that she was going to come in and dictate how everything should be done. Sex was at the heart of most of the exchange, triggering the sexual shame that had only worsened over the course of my relationship with R. Over the coming weeks there was an increasing amount of explosive anger and coercive control from J. If I didn't do something the way she wanted it done she would lash out in extreme ways and then punish me with days of hostile treatment.

Abuse

From these beginnings, the abuse in both relationships only escalated as the months and years passed. R's style of abuse consisted mostly of belittling, insulting, mocking and gaslighting me on a daily basis. Gaslighting is a form of manipulation that involves leading a person to doubt their own perception of reality. One example of the many smaller-scale instances of gaslighting is when I would try to push back against her insults. She would claim that she was only joking, that I had no sense of humor and then ridicule me for *that*. The next time she insulted me, I would question myself — am I just being too sensitive? Is she just being funny and I don't get it? That is the point of gaslighting; it is designed to get control over another person by making them doubt themselves, doubt their perception of reality. R's gaslighting was very much tied to her grandiosity and sense of entitlement. She would even tell me how I was feeling about things — "no, you're not feeling that, you're feeling this." Because I wasn't in touch with my emotions and habitually deferred to others, it was fairly easy to control me in this way.

Like me, R was busy building her own stories about our relationship, and because of her narcissism, it wasn't going to include any sort of personal responsibility on her part. It had to be me that was causing the inevitable issues that we experienced as a couple. She eventually decided that everything that was wrong with our relationship was because I lacked confidence and masculinity. She tapped into the entire pool of shame that I had already been carrying and easily convinced me that she was right. I had to make it a quest to get to the bottom of why I lacked confidence and masculinity. It would become a never-ending, soul-crushing fool's errand that would leave me more powerless and hopeless than ever. She reinforced this narrative every day with new rounds of condescending and contemptuous comments that nearly drove me to suicide. By the time I met J, R's daily abusive behaviors had trained me to doubt myself in every way. Fawning had become a way of life. Compliance was my only path to safety.

J's style of abuse was different from R's; her style involved regular angry outbursts filled with shouting, swearing, insults and threats. On the rare occasions anger didn't work or if she sensed it wouldn't work, she would fall back on guilt and manipulation. In the earlier days of the relationship, when she still felt the need to make excuses for her verbal violence, the abuse would often be followed by rationalizations: she felt tired, she felt sick, the people at her workplace were mean to her. We, meaning me, just needed to solve those problems and then she would treat me well.

J's ultra-controlling behaviors were ever present. She would express things in a way that amounted to "if you're going to be with me, this is how you're expected to behave," but then at the same time, it was expected that I would never leave. Some of her behaviors had lasting effects on me, like the way she would curse at me and pound the bed if I moved at all while she was trying to sleep. I became an extremely light sleeper, aware that any movement on my part would provoke an attack. She expected me to do things for her like drive her car or fold her laundry, then get angry and tell me I was doing everything wrong. Any time we had to leave the house, she would get extremely frazzled and lash out in some way. I was constantly walking on eggshells, and felt the need to be hypervigilant at all times in order to not upset her.

Trauma Bonds

For me, with my unhealed trauma, my history of responding to other people codependently, and my emotional avoidance, the narcissistic abuse was extremely difficult to navigate. There were times during both relationships when I felt suicidal. Like with my friendship with G, leaving the relationship with R never even crossed my mind. With J, I made an early attempt to break it off, but after hours of her crying, arguing and insisting that she was not going to "let me go," I settled in that relationship as well.

My system saw their behaviors as threats because they were threats. But the way I had taught myself to respond to interpersonal threats was to try to defuse them, to comply and fall in line. Fighting back didn't feel like an option, just as it didn't feel like an option when I was a young child navigating how to respond to my dad's angry outbursts or my friend G's attacks. Fleeing didn't feel like an option either, since I would sense the abuser would follow and continue the attack, which in fact is what usually happened. So I froze and I fawned, again and again, from one abusive episode to the next, in an endless, toxic cycle.

It's understandably confusing to witness an abusive relationship from the outside. Why would anyone accept abuse day after day and do nothing about it? Why would anyone stand by and allow mistreatment of others? How can these people live with themselves? As details emerge, it may start to make a bit more sense. Maybe the person being abused is afraid for their physical safety if they leave. Maybe they worry about how they'll get by without the abusive person in their lives. They may be fully aware of the situation, but feel alone, powerless and stuck. Even just reaching out for help is too much of a risk.

When it came to my relationships with R and J, it was not a matter of being aware and feeling stuck. It wasn't just a matter of being too afraid to act, although I had a lot of fear in those relationships. Then why did I stay? Certainly my codependent behaviors, my fear of disappointing people, the endless cycle of compliance and seeking of approval regardless of the cost to myself, played a role. My emotional avoidance also played a role. There was an additional mechanism at play in these two relationships, however, something called a trauma bond. Despite how it sounds, trauma bonding does not refer to the bond people form when they endure a trauma together. It is a term that describes how a person being abused can become inadvertently tied emotionally and psychologically to their abuser, making it that much more difficult to break free of the relationship. A common example is Stockholm syndrome, where a hostage winds up identifying and empathizing with their captor and supporting their goals. However this is just one example because a trauma bond can form in any type of abusive relationship.

How Trauma Bonds Form

What usually binds people together in an intimate relationship are things like mutual love and affection, shared goals and values, respect and care.

But instead, the bonds I experienced with both R and J were rooted in trauma. Their abusive behavior triggered my past trauma and activated the codependent habits that I had formed in response. As the relationships progressed, I endured additional emotional and psychological wounds that further incapacitated me and compromised my ability to break free from the trauma bonds.

For a trauma bond to form, there are two critical conditions to be met. First, there's a power imbalance; the person who is being abused feels as though the abuser has most or all of the control in the relationship, leading to feelings of helplessness. On paper, it looked like I had more power in the relationships with R and J. I was physically larger and stronger; I made more money; I was more educated and had more intellectual resources than they did. I didn't feel any of that power. I was used to doubting myself and deferring to others. I had convinced myself that I was powerless. This is why I was particularly vulnerable to narcissistic people, people who felt entitled to having all the control in a relationship and were ready to violently enforce that position.

The other condition that contributes to the trauma bond is the intermittent nature of the abuse. The abusive behaviors aren't constant — there are periods of calm and even care. This intermittency causes confusion for the person being abused, leading them to desperately seek out and hold onto those periods of calm. When an abusive episode ends and the period of calm begins, the person abused may even experience a release of chemical messengers in the brain, ones that influence how they experience pain, pleasure and reward, further clouding the situation.

The trauma bond in each of my romantic relationships had already started to form right from the first conversation. R and J felt entitled to their wants, needs and desires being prioritized, and I was already trained to do this. They expected validation, and I felt compelled to provide it. They needed their emotions to take center stage and I was ready to regulate them. They needed to feel control over everything and everyone around them, to feel powerful, and I was ready to turn over my power right from the start. I had to make these relationships work. The intermittent nature of the abuse kept me motivated to avoid words and behaviors that I perceived would lead to abuse, and to capitalize on the moments of calm in every way I could. Authenticity didn't matter, I was in survival mode.

I would find myself joining in with their rationalizations, excusing their behaviors towards others, as well as excusing abuse directed at me. They must be right — it must have been my fault. I just need to try harder next time. Every time I gave in and supported the narcissists' abusive behavior, it became that much more acceptable to them. I found that over time, they did less and less work rationalizing their behaviors, while at the same time increasing the level of denial.

Once the trauma bond was fully in place, it came to dominate my life. I accepted my abuser's reality and took it on as my own. The more difficult it got with R and J, the harder I would feel the need to try. The abusers became the most important people in my life, sucking up all of my emotional and intellectual resources.

Cognitive Dissonance

Right from the start, then throughout both of those relationships, I was faced with cognitive dissonance on a regular basis. Cognitive dissonance is a term for the state of discomfort that comes when a person has two or more thoughts that contradict each other. Everyone experiences this, and everyone needs to develop strategies for resolving those contradictions. Feeling cognitive dissonance can often wind up being positive experiences for people, if it leads them to challenging their beliefs and changing something about themselves or their life situation that isn't serving them.

During the earlier months of my relationship with R, conscious, confusing thoughts regularly popped into my head. An abusive episode would end and I would notice how the relationship felt nothing like what I had told myself I wanted when I was in the safety of my friendship with E. Similarly, I vividly remember a time when J had stormed out of the house after a particularly violent verbal attack and I found myself yelling at myself at the top of my lungs, "what the hell are you doing?" My response to these internal conflicts was always the same — rather than trying to resolve dissonance, I quickly dismissed the thoughts, tucked away the feelings, then later went on to justify what was happening and to stay the course at all costs.

I was doing the work of the abusers myself, even in between the abusive episodes. This was where most of the fawning came in. I was being trained on how to behave from the abusive episodes, and because of my codependency and habitual compliance, I was always looking for ways to do this work. What do I need to change about myself, whether I agree with the change or not? What lie do I need to tell these people to keep them calm, or even happy? I needed to believe these lies myself to some extent, for them to be believable, for them to stick.

When in those relationships, I was no longer a separate individual. My judgment was replaced by theirs, and I didn't have the capacity to imagine anything other than what each of them told me about who they were, who I was, and what the relationship meant. At no point did I take a step back to think about whether I was actually getting anything out of the relationship. Was I satisfied with my overall situation? Did I feel safe, cared for, understood? How did I really feel about each of them? Were they even the type of people I enjoyed interacting with? Were my days filled with doing things that engaged me, that excited me? Did I start my day and end my day fulfilled and excited to share my experiences with the person I was devoting my entire life to? I was too afraid to ask myself these types of questions, because part of me knew that I couldn't handle knowing the answer.

Instead of allowing myself to see the reality of what I was experiencing, I was fooling myself into believing I was there for legitimate reasons and that the relationships made sense. I felt the need to defend those relationships as if I was defending myself. If anyone came too close to the truth, I would feel shame and become defensive, resentful. I would occasionally complain about them to other people, but even then, I would offer a sanitized version of their behaviors. I was lying to myself, to R and J, and to everyone else on a daily basis about what was really happening, including what I actually felt about both of them. I had taken over the gaslighting, to where I was gaslighting myself.

Shame And Fear

Power imbalance and intermittent abuse established the bond — shame and fear strengthened and protected it. The sources of the fear and shame in those relationships resembled the sources from my childhood — the invalidation of my needs and desires, feeling unloved, feeling unable to protect myself or others. I excused R and J's bad behaviors as best I could — both the ones directed at me, and the ones directed at others. I became a sidekick to their mistreatment of others. Once again, I was the scared little boy who was standing slightly behind G, fake laughing while he abused other people, this time including people who were important to me.

I rationalized and told stories as a way to manage the constant fear, shame and cognitive dissonance that I was experiencing. But all this did was keep me suspended in a state of ignorance, leading to even more fear and shame. I then felt the overwhelming need to avoid that fear and shame too, creating a closed, self-perpetuating system. The ball of unresolved emotions that I was already carrying became larger and more unmanageable. As when I was younger, I suffered from depression and anxiety during those relationships, but those were treated like problems to be medicated, not signals that something was wrong with my life.

I'm not saying that I was just some innocent victim in these relationships. My behaviors were dishonest and self-seeking. I was inauthentic, resentful, and often controlling and manipulative in my own ways. Because so much of my emotional bandwidth was occupied by being on constant threat alert, I had a really hard time staying present, especially when being actively triggered, which I was on almost a continuous basis. I wasn't present for myself and I wasn't present for anyone else in my life. I was at full emotional capacity and it was difficult for me to empathize with others. My emotional signals were trying to alert me to these facts but my impulse was to avoid the signals and bury the fallout.

Relationship Endings

The trauma bond with R was incredibly strong and I was in a state of delusion. As far as I was concerned, it was a completely legitimate relationship that I was trying to fix by somehow becoming more confident and masculine. Everyone I knew seemed to be fully on board not only with the relationship, but with her. People I had known my entire life bought into her vision, not just of who she was, but how she had stepped in and made me a better person. I was full of unconscious shame that I was the one failing the relationship and fear of what that meant. I was afraid of her and ashamed of the way she treated me, but I was unable to sit with those emotions and incorporate them into an honest picture of my life and my experiences.

When R said she wanted a divorce, my first reaction was feelings of rejection, followed by more shame of failure. I was able to escape those feelings by distracting myself, mostly with thoughts of what I would do next, how I could now make decisions for myself on where I wanted to live and what to do with my days. I felt a sense of relief, but not because I would soon be free of daily abuse. I wasn't able to admit to myself that abuse was even part of my experience. Really, I was mostly experiencing relief that I would no longer need to be performing, and failing to perform, for R.

I was the one that eventually ended the relationship with J and asked for a divorce, but with very little agency on my part. J had asked for an open marriage, and in opening the relationship, a lot more people were able to observe J's behaviors first-hand. What I was working so hard at hiding from myself and other people, that this was an abusive, dysfunctional relationship with a narcissistic partner, was coming to light. The shame of being in that relationship was getting more and more difficult to avoid. Ultimately, the growing sense of shame I experienced about remaining in the relationship came to outweigh the fear of leaving it.

It was not easy to end the relationship with J. Even after I had decided to do so, I was terrified of actually going through with it. It was well beyond the usual fear I felt when faced with potentially disappointing someone. I couldn't even articulate what the fear was. Really, I could barely even admit to myself that it was even fear. As I often did, I was paralyzing myself with what-ifs. I was having fake conversations in my head about what to say if she replied in a certain way. I expected the conversation to resemble litigation in a court case, where I'd have to make my case as to why I wanted out. Any time the fear grew too intense, I found myself trying to sever my emotions and reduce it all to some kind of checklist of pros and cons — justifications for why I needed to leave the relationship, or why I was even entitled to.

Ultimately, the divorce conversation with J was much more spontaneous than I had imagined. She was trying to plan a future vacation and I was being noticeably awkward and hesitant. When she asked me what was going on, I said "I don't see a future for this relationship." Far simpler than I had planned, but it served its purpose and produced the expected result. She exploded. I then mostly just let her dump her anger, bitterness and guilt on me. I was in a freeze state and let her rage.

But I wasn't free of the trauma bond just yet. In some ways, it only got more intense. I still felt responsible for her. I still let her dictate how things would play out, what she was entitled to. She would remind me regularly that she didn't want the relationship to end, that she was owed some kind of compensation. Her controlling behaviors continued, in some ways getting worse, including threats and attacks. I was still full of fear and desperately searching for ways to escape with as little damage as I possibly could.

Not only was I still trapped with the effects of

the trauma bonds with R and J, the shame and trauma I was already carrying since childhood had compounded, adding several new layers. In some cases, those layers were quite a bit more intense, reaching areas of my life that trauma had yet to really affect, like sex or finances. My behaviors in response had correspondingly become more complex and deeply embedded.

CHAPTER 5: THE FULLY MADE CODEPENDENT MIND

I was in my mid-40's, with two failed marriages, carrying the heaviest load I had ever carried of unresolved trauma, shame, fear, resentment and sadness. I was in full self-preservation mode, ready to react the same way to perceived threats as I always had. I hadn't learned anything from those relationships.

Why was I in those marriages? Why did I stay when things were so obviously bad? Could I even admit that they were bad? Why were those relationships so similar in so many ways? What did I really feel about each of them? What did I feel about myself? What did I really know about myself? What did I desire out of life? What did I expect out of relationships? What was it going to take to break my pattern?

Even though I had spent decades avoiding my emotional signals, distorting them and rationalizing them beyond recognition, the signals kept coming. Even though I had been betraying myself by doing things I didn't want to do and associating with people I didn't even like, my authentic side was still always there, however much in the background, waiting for the life it deserved. It was at this point that I met Stephanie.

A Vision Of Another Life

Stephanie and I met in person at an event. We had an engaging first conversation. We were physically, emotionally and intellectually attracted to each other. We kept in touch. We started dating, and eventually fell in love. There was no love bombing, no moving in together within a few weeks, no rushing from one relationship milestone to the next. There was a genuine connection that deepened over time. It felt right, and it was right.

Stephanie was looking for an emotionally intimate relationship. So was I, ultimately, but I had lost touch with what that even meant by the time we started dating. Emotional intimacy would quickly prove difficult for me to handle, once we started down that road. I had unhealed trauma and layers of shame and fear to thank for that. I was carrying a lifetime of stories and narratives about myself and my life, along with everyone in it, past and present, and had no idea of how many holes, inconsistencies and flat-out lies were buried in those stories.

J still had access to me when Stephanie and I started dating. Not only had I not broken the trauma bond, she was still living in the house that I owned and we were still going through our divorce. All of the new layers of shame that led me to ask for the divorce were still very fresh and at the surface. I was still very much afraid of J and what she might do if I made one wrong move, said one wrong thing. I was equally afraid of staring into the face of shame for too long.

Stephanie started to notice some confusing behaviors. One minute I would be complaining about J and her treatment of me, the next I would be backpedaling and saying that things were mostly fine with that relationship. One minute I would be saying that I never wanted to speak to J again, the next I was answering her phone call to console her and tell her everything was going to be alright. I could sometimes acknowledge that J wasn't a good person and was taking advantage of me, yet when push came to shove, I would bend over backwards to accommodate and support her. There were numerous people in my life who were telling me that I needed to "kick her out and change the locks," but that suggestion did nothing but terrify me.

Naturally, none of this was adding up for Stephanie. As she started to ask questions, everything only got more and more confusing for both of us. There was no consistency to my stories about my relationship with J. The more it came to light about what my relationship with J was really like, who she was as a person, the types of things I did while I was with her, how I treated those around me like my family, the more difficult these exchanges between Stephanie and I started to get. At times I would completely freeze and lose my ability to speak for a period of time. When I managed to emerge from that state, I would blurt out the first thing that came to mind in an attempt to defuse the situation, to end the conversation. Sometimes I would tell flat-out lies. What was causing me to behave this way? Why was I responding with defensiveness to what was simply curiosity coming from someone I loved, who was trying to get to know me emotionally? It didn't seem to line up with the person I thought I was or the person Stephanie had fallen in love with.

It wasn't just bizarre, often hurtful exchanges or my struggle to make sense of my past that was causing problems. I seemed to lack intentionality much of the time. I acted as if things just happened to me. I struggled to articulate why I liked the things or people I liked or what I disliked. It often seemed as though I was just lining up, agreeing with everything, going along for the ride. I had difficulty explaining what I was feeling and how my feelings were connected to my actions.

Things needed to change, and I knew they needed to change, but I had no idea where to start. I was devouring all of the emotional energy in the relationship. Stephanie was doing too much of the emotional labor and it couldn't go on for much longer. But I desperately wanted this to work. I could feel at a profound level that I was where I was supposed to be — I just couldn't express it and day after day my ability to empathize would escape me. Another difficult conversation would start and once again, I'd be going down a shame spiral.

Despite my lack of self-awareness and my emotional immaturity, I did possess the willingness and motivation for growth. I was serious about getting to the bottom of these behaviors and committed to making regular efforts to figure out how to go about that. With consistent effort, I started to learn about myself and my past. Stephanie came across and suggested I read about the connection between codependency and narcissism. The realization that I was most likely codependent and that my previous partners, J and R, were most likely narcissists led to a whole new level of understanding. As I explored that particular toxic link, so many things started to make sense.

Even with that realization, the task before me seemed daunting. How was I going to get through all this? Was our relationship going to survive? There were times Stephanie wasn't sure that it would, and there were times I wasn't either. But I wasn't about to give up. There had to be answers. There had to be a way to heal, to change these behaviors, whatever they were. I started to approach it as if my life depended on it, because in many ways, it did.

PART TWO - THE RE-MAKING OF A CODEPENDENT MIND

CHAPTER 6: GETTING STARTED

Let's go back to the beginning for a moment. It's important to keep in mind that codependency is a set of learned behaviors. These behaviors were at one point strategic and adaptive. In situations where I had little to no power, the behaviors were meant to keep me safe. At some point, however, they became habitual and formed the template for how I navigated most or all interpersonal interactions or relationships. The good news is that behavior habits can be unlearned, reprogrammed.

Reprogramming my codependent behaviors wasn't about trying to remove unwanted behaviors. It wasn't even about trying to find and replace them with different, healthier behaviors. It was about shifting those behaviors from the dysfunctional versions to the functional versions. The re-making process started with awareness — where these particular versions of the behaviors came from, how they once served me, then how and when they became disordered. This is everything we explored in Part I.

Before reprogramming the behaviors there needed to be a clearing away of sorts. Betraying myself day after day took a major emotional toll. Painful emotions never got resolved. Shame, fear and resentment built up over time and the load got heavier and heavier. Carrying this load took a tremendous amount of emotional energy and made it extremely difficult to see things clearly. In order to gain the necessary self awareness, I had to face all of those unresolved emotions.

It was extremely difficult and often painful work. I had to acknowledge and confront emotions that I'd been avoiding for the majority of my life. I was avoiding those emotions for a reason — they felt unsafe and I didn't trust that I could handle them. I thought I was doing what was best for myself. Once I started on this work, the temptation to fall back into these behaviors was extremely strong, especially when I was confronted with the most painful feelings of all, like shame.

Motivation

A question that I asked myself a number of times

during the process — is all of this painful work worth it? Is it really better on the other side? Having made it to the other side, I will say with all of my heart that yes, it is worth it. I would go through it again and again if I had to, to have what I have now and be who I am now. When I say "other side," I don't mean that I'm 100% cured and no codependent or shame-based behaviors ever come up — they do. But I understand myself now. I know the behaviors when I see them, and I course-correct. I know what was causing my depression and anxiety. My eyes are open and even though things aren't always going to go perfectly all the time, I have confidence that I won't revert back to the way I was: that is, close my eyes, start avoiding all of my painful emotions, and cater to the needs of the most demanding person in my orbit.

Of course a big part of why I can say it's worth it is because I'm now in the type of relationship I know deep down I always wanted. A relationship that has emotional intimacy, safety, sexual satisfaction, autonomy, excitement and of course love. I can incorporate everything I know about myself and this other human being into a big picture view of my life and finally look at my whole life, including my future. I feel a clarity about who I am and the decisions I make, and my emotions tell me every day that I'm in the right place with the right person. There's very little confusion — nothing like the kind I used to have, anyway. There is always going to be fear of loss, miscommunications, differing opinions or needs — that's part of being vulnerable, and being separate, autonomous individuals. But I understand my fears now too. My emotions are no longer a jumbled mess.

So where did I start, when it came to this transition — the re-making of my codependent mind? Well the whole point of shifting away from my codependent behaviors was so that I could have stronger relationships with other people. I wasn't going to make these changes in isolation. I had to make honest attempts at connecting with other people.

Getting Help

I tried the therapy route a handful of times — once before I met R, then three more times during that relationship, including intensive group therapy. In every case, the experiences failed to provide me with an understanding of my past experiences or offer an effective strategy to deal with struggles that I was having. I think the main reason for this failure was that I was bringing the wrong information to the therapists and I had the wrong goals. I was essentially just looking for relief from my symptoms. How can I overcome depression and anxiety? How can I feel better about myself and gain self-confidence? These therapists didn't know me, so all they had to work with was what I brought them. It's very possible that one of those therapists could have gotten there eventually, but I wasn't willing to spend that much time making what felt to me like no progress.

One of the biggest failures of the therapy experience for me, though, was that nobody managed to recognize the abusive nature of my relationship with R, even when I was spending three hours a day, three times a week in a group therapy setting. This failure may have been, in part, due to the unfortunate fact that people still have a tendency to downplay the severity of emotional abuse. Then on top of that, there could have been some gender dynamics at play, where any abusive behaviors that I was reporting were being downplayed even further because I was a man being abused by a woman. I do think it's possible, as well, that I was very good at spinning stories to make it seem as though everything was my fault and R only meant well.

The worst therapy experience I had was when R and I went to a couples counselor. Despite the counselor actually using the word "abusive" when describing R's behaviors, the abuse was quickly dismissed; the rest of the therapeutic experience became about validating R's narrative and getting to the bottom of how to make me more confident and masculine. It was humiliating and sent me even further in the wrong direction, leading me right into another abusive relationship with J. I can't emphasize this enough — people in an abusive relationship don't need couples counseling. They need to be free from that relationship in order to heal. Once I was with J, I didn't even try therapy at all.

I don't want to sound too discouraging about the potential benefits of individual or group therapy. Just because I didn't have positive experiences, doesn't mean others don't or can't. Things could have been very different for me if I had gone with more knowledge about myself from the start. It would have been helpful if I understood a little about the trauma I experienced as a child, and brought that to a trauma-informed therapist. While short-term goals like pulling out of severe depression can be important, spending too much time focusing on my symptoms like depression or low self-esteem didn't get me any closer to healing. I needed to focus on discovering the root causes for the behaviors that kept me repeating dysfunctional patterns. I definitely feel that if I went equipped with at least a little awareness of my trauma and codependent behaviors, I would have set very different goals and been able to establish a more effective connection with a therapist.

There are plenty of other options that I could have tried along the way as well, or at least given more of a chance. If I understood anything about codependency, I could have given 12 step programs like Co-Dependents Anonymous or Al-Anon a try. As I mentioned in the first chapter, I did attend one meeting of Co-Dependents Anonymous during my relationship with R but neither the way codependency was explained nor the suggested path for recovery resonated with me. But regardless of the specifics of the CoDA program, I could have benefited from regular interaction with other people trying to navigate interpersonal relationships. I could have also spent more time researching online, reading books or finding other online communities to interact with. I was buried deep in my codependent behaviors, and also heavily distracted by all of the emotional avoidance. I was on the complete wrong path. I didn't know what I was working with or how to ask for help.

Connecting With Other People

Despite being unable to access help through formal channels like therapy and support groups, other people would still prove critical in breaking my codependency cycle. I did not have much skill or experience with either finding people to connect with, or turning casual acquaintances into deeper relationships. Additionally, for the majority of the time I was in the relationships with R and J, I was mostly isolated and kept myself isolated. There were times in both of those relationships however, when I was putting myself in social situations, meeting people, and making myself more authentically and emotionally available. Other people were able to get a closer look at my situation, my toxic partners and my experiences with those partners first-hand. I fell short of going deep enough with anyone at the end of the relationship with R, though, and went right back into the thick of codependency with J. But by the end of my relationship with J, I had found a handful of people who I really started to connect with. That's when things started to finally move in the right direction.

Extracting myself from the abusive relationship with J was extremely difficult, and a huge hurdle to get over, but a necessary one. I had to recognize and embrace that I did not deserve that kind of treatment — no matter what stories I may have told myself to excuse it. It wouldn't have been possible for me to begin healing or understanding myself while my codependent habits were being activated by J's abuse. The trauma bond that was still in place made being honest with myself especially hard to do. Breaking that trauma bond got exponentially easier when I started to open up to people about what I was experiencing and was able to accept their support and assistance.

Having other people in my life as I was ending my marriage to J forced me to start to confront the truth of that relationship. Additionally, more eyes on the situation meant more accountability on my part; I needed to take the actions that I said were important to my health and happiness. And perhaps most critically, the friendships I was forming provided motivation for me to make changes. I was feeling an investment in other people, and those people were feeling an investment in me. It was becoming more clear what I would lose by continuing along the same destructive path.

Chief among the people who I connected with at the end of my relationship with J was Stephanie. Our relationship established the building blocks for the eventual shift in my codependent behaviors. I talked about the ways in which we started to make certain connections in the previous chapter, realizations that pointed us in the right direction — but there were some key factors that I think set us up for success. We were in love, for starters, which gave us motivation to get to the bottom of what was becoming more and more of an urgent problem between us — my codependency and emotional immaturity. She got to know me well enough to know when I was lying, or at least giving up too easily with explanations that didn't quite add up. She wasn't afraid to express when I said or did things that were hurtful to her, while still managing to hold onto her empathy for me in the process.

Essentially what I found in Stephanie was someone who was invested in me, someone who was committed to knowing me and someone who was ready to challenge me. If I didn't have Stephanie, those are the qualities I would look for in a therapist. In all honesty, it may have been easier to do some of the work with a therapist. Many of our difficult discussions were made all the more difficult because of the stakes involved. There were a number of times our relationship was put at risk as we both struggled to process painful emotions and to navigate situations in which our emotional needs were at odds. I feel very lucky to have found Stephanie, but I believe that I could have also got to where I am now with the help of a therapist or a supportive group, had I been equipped with just a little bit of knowledge of what I was up against.

Journaling

In addition to help from other people, another element that has been critical to my healing is journaling. It has been hugely helpful for me to set aside time to reflect on my life — past, present and future. I've found that writing focuses my thoughts and gives me something to refer back to as I flesh out who I was and who I wanted to be going forward.

My writing has taken on several different forms over the years, but I started small. At first, it was a very basic daily journal where I answered a set of questions about the day. Very quickly, however, just answering the same questions every day became not enough. There were too many things that I still didn't understand about myself, especially my past and how I became the way I was. At that point I decided to carve out an hour or more every weekday, and some weekend days, to really start to dig into my past and see what I could learn. This was right around the time that Stephanie had suggested I look into codependency and narcissism.

I found it useful to time what I came to call my "reflection hour" to immediately precede a discussion hour with Stephanie. The two of us spent many of those end-of-day connections sitting and talking about the things I was learning about myself, as well as navigating our relationship and what it meant. A very regular occurrence, especially in the beginning, but still to this day, would be to go over what came up in my writing sessions. The next day, I would then go back and edit what I wrote the previous day, before moving on to the next subject. It took a while for me to learn how to connect my emotions to the process of analyzing my past, so the potential explanations I came up with often fell short, or wound up being completely off in certain ways. Stephanie would help me to dissect it all, driven by her own curiosity and investment in getting to the bottom of things.

I went on to write quite a bit more, as I continued the daily reflection process, and we continued to have those discussions. This combination of spending chunks of time reflecting on myself with running those thoughts by another person is what has made progress possible for me.

CHAPTER 7: HEALING TRAUMA AND EMOTIONAL WOUNDS

Doing this work was often a very painful process for both Stephanie and myself. It sometimes felt like one step forward, two steps back, especially in the earlier days. It could have gone more smoothly if we were aware of certain things earlier in the process. For example, it would have been easier for both of us if I had understood how and when my trauma was involved in our conversations, and if I was able to recognize and process my emotions. Instead, I went right into reflecting on my past, both recent and distant, and began to have an extremely difficult time emotionally. I had no understanding of the trauma that I was carrying and what it looked like or felt like when I reacted to that trauma. I was also still habitually avoiding my emotions. It was risky and it was messy. So while my understanding of trauma, trauma responses and trauma triggers, actually came later in my healing process, I think it is best to start with a discussion of what I eventually learned and have since incorporated.

How Threat Responses Become Trauma Responses

When I was a small child my dad's anger felt like a threat to me, as did my mother's distress and depression. Fighting or fleeing was not an option for me. The freeze and fawn responses were the only ones available and that's how my body became conditioned to respond to threats. When I met my abusive friend G, that conditioning was fully activated. When I was being verbally or physically assaulted, I froze, let it happen, and waited for it to be over. Once the attack was over, I would go into fawn mode, to do everything I could to try to keep him from attacking me again, for as long as I possibly could. It didn't ever occur to me that I could flee (by leaving the friendship) or fight back, even if it were just to tell my parents or teachers what was happening.

The abuse itself, the experiences of the abuse, combined with my responses - these were getting stored in my body. Subconsciously, I was becoming more and more practiced at recognizing when the next round of abuse was coming and anticipating it so that I could more quickly deploy the freeze or fawn response. Going forward, if I experienced anything that my body interpreted as a similar interpersonal threat, whether it was truly a threat or not, it would produce the same physiological responses, sending me back into those original experiences.

Instead of an adaptive threat response, one that would optimize my chance at safety, I was experiencing a trauma response. Trauma had hijacked my ability to respond to certain types of threats in effective ways. Rather than responding to an actual threat (which sometimes it may be, of course), I would wind up responding more to an idea, a kind of muscle memory — a phantom threat. I wasn't able to assess the threat potential head-on, since the trauma I had experienced had been attached to the feeling of threat.

Freezing and fawning as a response to abusive behavior isn't a good long-term or permanent solution. If there is an angry or entitled person demanding something from me, freezing, fawning and giving the person what they want may solve the immediate problem, but will create much bigger problems down the road. It's likely going to lead to people taking advantage of me over and over again and make it difficult for me to leave relationships and situations that are unhealthy for me. As well, I would perceive these threats in behaviors that were not abusive like someone disagreeing with me, and respond in similar ways. I was both inadvertently tying myself to abusive people who took advantage of my freezing and fawning behaviors and building a wall between me and everyone else, when it came to establishing emotional intimacy.

Trauma Triggers

What triggers a trauma response can be complex and nuanced, and will look different for everyone. As well, not everything that triggers a threat response will trigger a trauma response. I can experience a threat, say an aggressive dog running at me, my trauma won't get triggered and I can respond appropriately — by fleeing. For me, it's in interpersonal spaces where I am most likely to be triggered. When I perceive something as interpersonally threatening, my body is sent back into my stored traumatic experiences, overriding my ability to respond in an adaptive way. I re-experience the trauma to some degree, and respond the same way as I did to survive the original situation.

Other peoples' negative emotional reactions have been the most common triggering experience for me. It is unpleasant for most people to witness other people's negative emotions, their anger, or disappointment or sadness. We are social creatures and it is perfectly natural, normal and healthy to have a physiological response to emotional displays by other people. For me, though, I feel implicated in those emotions. When I was initially traumatized, those emotions were forced on me, they were made my responsibility. Along with that feeling of responsibility came powerlessness, because I never felt as though there was anything I could really do — hence the freezing and fawning. Then, any time I experience any level of powerlessness, shame is quick to follow — the most painful emotion of all for me.

Once the trauma response chain reaction is triggered, I've entered what resembles a threat response in that I go into survival mode. Emotional processing is interrupted, empathy is severed and I go into a state of self-preservation. Because the experience is clouded by trauma, my available responses are severely limited. My main goal in those moments is to search for the quickest way to survive the situation. Since I already taught myself at an early age which behaviors seemed to work the best to keep me safe, I would just default to those.

Recognizing Trauma Responses

I stumbled into recognizing my trauma responses about a year into the daily reflections and discussions with Stephanie about codependency. The conversation took a familiar, but uncomfortable turn — Stephanie was expressing curiosity about my emotional life and I wasn't sure how to respond. I was quickly hit with a wave of fear of how it would look to not have a ready answer, followed by the shame of what that meant. That fear and shame then immediately tapped into the pool of fear and shame I was already carrying and exploded into a much deeper feeling of panic. The panic then led to emotional flooding, which is a term for when a person becomes overwhelmed by stress hormones, sending the person into threat mode. This cascade of emotional reactions came upon me quickly and automatically. This particular instance was severe enough to send me into a freeze state.

Freeze responses for me are extremely terrifying and frustrating. I feel like I do in dreams when I'm trying to run away from something, but my body isn't responding. My brain is like static on an old TV and I feel like I'm going to explode. I have a desperate need to say something, but I can't. Words won't even come to my mind, let alone out of my mouth. It's an extremely helpless feeling, which brings on another wave of fear and shame. In the past, a common way I would pull myself out of a freeze state is to bring in resentment towards the person I perceived as having caused the experience.

Resentment shifts the power dynamic just enough in my head so that I can then respond. At this point, I've lost sight of the actual conversation. I've severed myself from any empathy for the other person, and I'm responding from a place of trauma. The goal is to survive the experience, which for me would involve defaulting to fawning behaviors. I would blurt out whatever I think might defuse the situation, shift focus, or change the subject. I might say something that sounded like it could be right, or I might flat-out lie. If that doesn't immediately work, I would get defensive and the cycle would continue until I reach safety.

In the case of the conversation with Stephanie when I became conscious that I was having a trauma response, freeze, and around the time when resentment entered the picture, I somehow managed to realize that I wasn't actually under threat. Stephanie wasn't attacking me; she wasn't shaming me. What was I actually afraid of here? Why was I feeling resentment? The state I was in was still very intense, but I paused just long enough to tune into what was actually happening around me and in my body. That awareness gave me just enough pause to allow me to re-engage with Stephanie from a calmer, less triggered state.

Since that realization, I've come to learn that it is almost exclusively during interpersonal exchanges that I experience trauma responses. I know now that those are the times when I need to be especially alert for signs that I might be triggered. I've also spent time reflecting on how I respond to different types of emotions from other people. It's okay to feel implicated in people's emotional responses in general, that's what empathy is; the problem is when that implication feels to me like judgment, disapproval, or a direct attack. Basically, when those emotional displays resemble what I experienced as a child and felt defenseless against them, that's when a trauma response is triggered.

Handling Trauma Responses

So what do I do when I find myself experiencing a trauma response? One important thing I've found is to try to avoid getting too discouraged when they happen. I may experience these to some degree for a really long time, if not the rest of my life. That doesn't mean there's something wrong with me as a human being. When I've felt that discouragement, it typically would include feelings of shame. I've had to learn to evaluate shame signals and understand when they are valid versus when they are misleading or false signals. The fact that I have trauma responses is not shameful. This is a physiological response coming from my body in response to something that got encoded a long time ago. What can wind up being shameful, however, are the ways in which I've behaved during some of the trauma responses. Those shame signals are there for a reason - they're telling me that my behavior was inappropriate, selfish, hurtful, negligent, whatever it may be.

With these things in mind, what has been most helpful when I experience a trauma trigger has been being able to recognize it and name it in the first place. When one does happen, it can become intense really quickly, and the reflexive reactions will be quick to follow. Reflecting on trauma responses I experienced in the past, how they felt and how I reacted, has given me the tools to recognize when I'm faced with a new one. Naming the trauma response as it starts has introduced a new element to the experience - awareness. With this awareness comes a pause, almost like a short-circuit in the progression of the response.

An important piece of awareness that I have worked on is to take a step back and think about where I am and who I'm interacting with. I ask myself if this particular situation or person is usually something or someone that I find safe? Is this an abusive person? Is it possible that I really am under attack, or is it more likely a false signal?

While it isn't always the case, it is sometimes necessary for me to take a pause. It may be a short pause, where I let the person know that I'm not quite sure how to respond and would like to think about it for a minute. Sometimes a longer pause is necessary, and I express the need to table the conversation until a later time. The purpose of the pause is not to come up with a satisfactory answer to whatever it is that caused the shame or fear; it is to create space for how to proceed. I'm not pausing or delaying the conversation to avoid the topic, as was the case in the past. Once I am aware that I'm experiencing a trauma response, and I understand the source, I have a greater chance of making better decisions about how to respond. Again, the goal is to be able to respond from a calmer, more emotionally informed position, rather than from a flooded, triggered position.

When navigating a trauma response, I've also found it helpful to focus on my breathing. I've noticed that when stressed, I have a tendency to breathe with much more shallow, short breaths, contributing to the feelings of panic. Deep breaths help calm me down. Additionally, if I notice that I've already started acting defensively or am feeling resentment at all, it helps to look at that with curiosity. If I know that I'm actually in a safe situation with a person who means me no harm, then it helps to try to bring empathy back into the equation, to not only be curious about what I'm feeling, but be curious about what they're feeling. I try to ask, if it's not clear.

With practice and lived experience, I've found that navigating my way through a trauma trigger can happen just as quickly and automatically as the trauma response progression itself. Once awareness is involved, the reactions or behaviors that come next are far less reflexive. Sometimes, I find that I still feel intense urges to react the same way as I used to, but that's completely understandable given that I've been responding the same way to shame for decades. Responding in a new way isn't an overnight shift.

Emotional Development

As I explored in Part I of this book, I learned very early on in my life that some emotions were mostly off limits to me. The painful emotions felt unsafe — anger, fear, shame — I didn't trust my ability to process or express them. Instead, I found as many ways as I could to try and avoid them or stuff them somewhere where I wouldn't have to deal with them. Of course they didn't actually go anywhere. I didn't resolve them and move forward with more self-awareness and confidence. Instead, I kept lumping them all together into this ball of unresolved emotions. They all got muddled and indistinguishable from each other. The longer they lurked around, the more afraid of them I became. Any time I would be reminded of any of them somehow, especially when experiencing a trauma response, it was as though I felt them all at once, and I would try that much harder to bury them deeper.

Looking back to that first year or so of this work, I can clearly see how I was still afraid of my emotions. I often left them out when doing my journaling and reflection or when having conversations with Stephanie. I wasn't necessarily compartmentalizing anymore, since I wasn't experiencing nearly as many things that I felt the need to compartmentalize, but I continued to avoid truly facing my emotions head-on. I was still having regular trauma responses and would often wind up feeling some version of shame, followed by moments of resentment and poor behavior to protect myself. So equally important as becoming aware of my trauma triggers and how my responses to them looked and felt, was developing an understanding of the emotions that I was feeling. I needed to be able to interpret my emotions in those moments of pause, in order to learn how to handle them differently.

As I previously discussed, emotions are there to provide us with valuable information about what's going on around us, and are there to guide us. Some emotions are going to be more painful and some will be more pleasurable. Some are going to give us useful, accurate information; some are going to be false signals, leading us down a wrong path. Our emotions need to be identified, so that we can make these distinctions and act from a more informed place. I think it's useful to think about emotional signals the same way I do physical signals, like hunger, thirst, fatigue or pain. My body is alerting me that something needs attending to. I listen to those signals. Physical signals aren't always clear or accurate either, but I pause to notice the signals and I go from there. I don't feel pain in my foot and keep on running because I'm afraid to face the fact that my foot hurts.

When I first started trying to look at and identify my emotions, I found that I had to pretty much start from scratch. I needed to learn to name what I was feeling and to separate out the various emotions, instead of lumping them all together. The more specific I can get during any particular moment, the better. Shame, guilt and embarrassment are all different emotions. Anger, frustration and irritation are different emotions. It has helped me to look up how others have described certain feelings to see if those descriptions and the associated named emotion makes sense with what I'm feeling. It's like building my vocabulary, but one that is directly linked to what's going on inside my body.

In addition to learning to identify my emotions, I had to get comfortable sitting with them for longer than a few seconds or a few minutes. Sitting with emotions involves allowing myself to feel them and move through them, rather than trying to suppress or go around them. These are the moments when I listen to and reflect on what they're telling me before I choose how to act. Sitting with emotions has sometimes been very difficult. Particularly, not surprisingly, the painful ones that I had been avoiding most of my life. I needed to build the capacity to move through those painful emotions, so I could trust myself to be able to handle it again and again. Every time I did so — every time I allowed myself to feel shame for an extended period of time, for instance — I was building that capacity. It started to become more natural for me to do it again, the next time I felt a painful emotion.

The more I sit with my emotions on a consistent basis, the more I am able to choose more effective responses to those emotions. I can think about what caused the emotion and what would be an appropriate response. When doing so, I have a much better chance of responding in a way that will actually keep me safe, or keep those around me safe. For example, I may be feeling anger because I'm being unjustifiably attacked by someone, or someone else is being similarly attacked. In that situation, feelings of anger might motivate me to take action in an attempt to correct the situation. Sometimes I'll feel conflicting emotions along with anger, like fear. That's a signal too, and that's okay, but I need to acknowledge that fear, so I can assess whether or not the fear is useful in that situation, or if it's just holding me back from an appropriate response to the anger.

The more I am able to identify and interpret my emotions, the easier it gets. The more I find myself responding from a place of awareness and being satisfied with the outcome, the more confident I become, and the more I'm able to trust myself. The outcome isn't always going to be perfect, of course, but I can be content that I at least behaved in a way that was more informed, less reactionary.

My ultimate goal is to process my emotions real-time. I try to incorporate them into my experiences as they happen, as much as possible, so there's less room for distortions or post-hoc rationalizations. It's not always easy. I doubt it is easy for anyone, even people who have had a lifetime of practice. Emotions are not always perfectly clear and the appropriate actions won't always be clear. Competing emotions can sometimes be difficult to reconcile. I understand this and I try not to judge myself too harshly if I'm less than perfect.

Having done the work of reconnecting with my emotions, I've found that I have much more power over my feelings, as opposed to them having power over me. I still experience painful emotions on a regular basis, including ones that resemble depression and anxiety. But I can usually quickly identify the source of those feelings and make a conscious choice of how to respond. At the same time, I'm able to more fully feel the pleasurable emotions. I can act with more authenticity and intentionality. And because I'm able to better manage my own emotional experiences, that has freed up my emotional capacity to be more present and empathetic with other people. Not only have I gained power over my own emotions, I've found that other people's emotions have less power over me at the same time.

CHAPTER 8: REWRITING STORIES

Telling stories is something we all do. It is an inherent part of what it means to be human, to participate in a human community. In their ideal form, stories help us understand ourselves and our world; they help us build lives of meaning and purpose; they connect us with other people. In their corrupted form, they do the opposite — they help us hide from ourselves and the world, becoming elaborate systems of evasion designed to shield us from other people and the reality of our lives.

Like everyone, my life was filled with various stories. There were stories that I picked up from other people: my family, my friends, the larger communities in which I lived. Then there were ones I constructed; there were stories about myself — who I saw myself to be and how I got that way. There were ones I told about other people — who I saw them as, how I experienced their behaviors and how those behaviors affected me. I also had stories about specific experiences. Many of these stories I would group together into larger, overarching narratives. In some cases, I wasn't necessarily too attached to a particular story; in other cases, I held on to some stories as if my life depended on it. If anyone called one of the latter stories into question, I would feel attacked, and I would defend the story as if I were defending myself.

Most of the stories and the larger narratives that I carried were not effective in helping me understand myself and the world, in building a life of meaning and purpose or in connecting me with other people. Not because they weren't based on fact, they usually were to some extent. But those facts were highly curated. I would only let in the information I needed to in order to make the story plausible to myself and other people. So in that way, they may or may not have been factual, but they certainly weren't true.

As I looked back at various stories from my life, I found one story after another that included some element of dishonesty. I'm not talking about errors in memory, like minor details or order of events, but what amounted to flat-out fabrications. A big reason for the stories that I wrote about myself and my life was in order to avoid the emotions that I was experiencing at the time. I kept my emotions out of the process as much as I could because they were telling me things that I didn't want to hear. Essentially, my stories were just rationalizations and were almost always formed after the fact, rather than arising directly from the situations themselves. I'm not talking about every experience I've ever had, just ones in which I found myself unable to handle the situation emotionally.

When faced with an emotionally difficult situation, I would go through a series of steps in order to successfully store the event in a way I could more easily handle. First, my emotions would be temporarily set aside and I would move through the situation in some form of freeze or fawn mode, just paying attention to the biggest threats and focusing on how to defuse them. Once things calmed down, I would then move in with the post-hoc explanations and rationalizations. If what I came up with seemed plausible enough, I would then take it on as my official explanation of what happened.

Shame

This way of dealing with challenging emotional situations, that is, dissociate during and then rationalize afterwards, produced stories that were riddled with shame landmines. There was the shame from the incident itself and whatever actually happened in the moment, including any fear or powerlessness I felt. There was the shame from creating a false story to try to avoid the reality of what happened. Finally, there was the shame from continuing to carry that story, telling it to myself and others, despite my emotions signaling that what I was saying wasn't the full truth, or worse, completely fabricated.

My storytelling ability had its limits and could only do so much in terms of containing and neutralizing these shame landmines. Regularly, I would find myself enlisting other people to navigate this dangerous territory. I've come to call this "shame venting." The way it looked was like this: I would be having a conversation with someone, or having a shared experience with someone, and my subconscious would be reminded of one of these shame-filled experiences from my past. I would quickly become consumed by those feelings of shame and wind up blurting out something related to that story, in an attempt to relieve or *vent* some of that shame. The things I would say ranged from benign statements that just seemed odd and pointless, all the way up to insensitive, poorly timed, overly-revealing, or even hurtful statements. I would have no idea what I was doing or why I was doing it. The person I shame-vented to would often be similarly confused.

Not only did I have a large amount of shame-filled stories that I was carrying, I had woven those stories into narratives. In my younger years, those narratives were about myself, that I was uninteresting or unattractive. Eventually I came to carry narratives that I suffered from depression, had low self-esteem and lacked confidence. Then there were the narratives I formed around the various relationships I was in, like the two toxic romantic relationships. Those narratives included stories designed to convince myself and others that they were legitimate relationships, worthy of my time and emotional energy.

These stories and narratives not only kept me stuck in cycles of shame-avoidance, they kept me ignorant about who I really was and what my life experiences really meant. They also kept everyone who was worth knowing in my life at a distance. Like my codependent behaviors, the stories were a block to intimacy. I needed to start to uncover what had actually happened, so that I could finally start to truly process my experiences, in a way that was going to lead to actual self-awareness. I needed to rewrite the stories and narratives of my life. In a way, it was as if I was un-compartmentalizing.

The Process

So how did I go about rewriting my various stories and narratives? For one, I started small, with individual stories, rather than trying to go straight for the narratives, which were much more complex. Without understanding at least some of the stories that went into those narratives, I would get quickly overwhelmed and the reflex would be to make up another false narrative to replace the original false one. It was very difficult to go straight from saying that my relationship with J was "fine," for example, to saying that she was a terrible person and the relationship was toxic. I certainly tried, but would be met regularly with cognitive dissonance. If that was true, then why was I there to begin with? Before I could really make sense of those false narratives, I needed to actually find and reflect on the various stories that made up that narrative. In the case of the relationship with J, that meant looking at the various pieces that made up that relationship. Why did I think it was fine? What were the stories, the experiences that went into that perception and what were the stories and experiences I was leaving out? Those were the ones I needed to start with to get to the bottom of what was really happening and what I was really feeling at the time.

In order to rewrite a story, I've found that I need to put myself back into the situation where the story came from, as best I can. I need to place myself there. It works best when I can be in a quiet, relaxed state — almost a meditative state. I've noticed it doesn't really matter how I feel at the time — I've had just as much success going into it feeling positive and hopeful as I do when I go into it feeling something like shame. Although when I first started doing this, the more positive the better, since it took a while for me to clear away those layers of shame and free up some emotional capacity. Especially since I was almost certainly going to feel more waves of shame revisiting those stories. I found that sticking to specific times to do this work helped too.

When revisiting the source of a past story, I think of as many details as I can, to help place myself there — the physical location of the experience, what it looked like, where I was standing or sitting, what the other person looked like, what they were saying, how they were saying it. No matter how hard I try, some details are not recoverable, despite this exercise — specific words that were said, for example. Some of those details may not have been stored at all to begin with, if I wasn't fully present and was in a triggered state. But this is where focusing on what I was feeling at the time comes in — what emotions were present. Even though I did my best to avoid the emotions I was feeling in those moments, all they did was get filed away in my ball of unresolved emotions. They were still there, ready for me to rediscover. In recovering the emotions, not only do I learn about what I was really feeling at the time, some of the seemingly lost details come into focus.

After reconstructing the situation as best I can, I reflect on how I behaved versus how I would have wanted to behave, given my current understanding of myself. Was I true to myself, or was I behaving codependently? Did I walk away with an authentic emotional reaction, or did I avoid what I was feeling, compartmentalize it and retell it to pretend I was feeling something completely different? As I do this, I'm rewriting the story to be a more truthful account of what happened. Then I can incorporate that more honest story into a new understanding of myself. What were the types of situations that caused me to behave codependently and avoid my emotions? What may still cause me to do this? These are vital pieces of information that have helped me in the process of growing and reprogramming my old behaviors.

Like most of the steps in the transition process, rewriting the stories of my past has been much more effective when I include other people in the process. Those people need to be willing and able to challenge me though, and not just validate everything I say, or it's not all that different from going at it alone. Stephanie has been especially helpful in this process not just because she had that ability to challenge me, but because she had first-hand knowledge of some of the stories I was trying to rewrite. When recounting stories of my relationship with J or with my family, for instance, she would often help add details I missed, or correct some of the ways in which I remembered certain things. She also would act as a second set of eyes, looking at those stories from a high level and when something didn't seem to add up or make sense, pressing me for additional information or clarification. Therapists, friends, family — as long as these people are safe connections, can play this role.

Rewritten Stories

There must be hundreds of stories I told myself throughout my life that fed my narratives, but there are a couple that I'll use here to help illustrate how the rewriting process looked. One is an experience I had in my early teenage years while at a week-long boy scout summer camp. There was a guy, M, who I was sort of friends with who became especially condescending, patronizing and aggressive towards me during the week. Any time I tried to push back, he would escalate with mocking and belittling behaviors, and attempt to enlist anyone who was around to join in, including my brother and one of my brother's friends. Whenever this happened, my brother sided with M, sometimes even adding his own mocking responses. The whole experience was making me feel extremely rejected, alone and overwhelmed with shame.

On the bus ride home from the trip, M had some candy and was offering it to the other kids, but when I got up to see if he would give me a piece, he yelled "not you!!" That was the last straw, and I went to the front of the bus, sat down and began to cry. M started making fun of me for crying and once again, my brother and his friend joined in. When we got home, I went to my brother to try to figure out what went wrong. Since everyone seemed to be against me, I figured it had to be me. I asked him why nobody liked me, what I was doing wrong. He said it was because I was being too argumentative and confrontational in my responses to M's treatment of me. People don't like when you challenge them, so I needed to stop doing that if I wanted people to like me. I took the advice to heart and made a conscious, almost relentless attempt to be as agreeable as possible. If I disagreed with someone, I kept it inside. If I didn't like someone's behavior, I kept it to myself and did everything I could to keep on that person's good side. My brother and I both considered making these *improvements* one of my finest achievements. The story that he and I would both tell was that I came to him, he gave me good advice, I learned something about myself and put my mind to making a positive change.

The story was useful in several ways. It got me out of the shame of being mistreated by my brother and people I thought were my friends. It also bypassed any anger I felt about how I was treated and the fear that came from the thought of acting on that anger. The story also fed at least two larger narratives that I carried. One being that my brother and I were close growing up, that he was my "best friend." The other narrative was that I was good at taking constructive criticism and making appropriate changes to myself.

It wasn't until decades later when I told Stephanie that story that it started to fall apart. This a perfect example of how involving other people in the rewriting process is helpful. As I described M's behaviors, she suggested that what was actually happening was that he was bullying me. I had every right to be angry, and regardless of what my behaviors were specifically at the time, that anger was justified. As we talked more about it, it became clear that the solution to that situation should have been to stop hanging out with M, not train myself to pacify him. I should have also questioned the nature of my relationship with my brother. Instead, I learned the complete opposite of what I needed to learn from that experience. Not only did it feed the false narratives I was building, it went to further fuel the depth and severity of my codependent behaviors.

The other story I'll describe here is one that involved shame that was actually appropriate for me to feel, that I nonetheless avoided the same way I avoided all shame. There was a 4th of July costume party at a local bar that J and I decided to attend. The theme was to wear something patriotic. J came up with the idea that we should pay tribute to the original inhabitants of America by dressing up like Native Americans. We bought some cheap headdresses online, put paint on our faces and taped signs on our back that had a slogan that was meant to honor Native American land rights. J also added ribboned arm bands and for some reason, a colorful tutu and hot pants with the British flag printed on them. It didn't occur to me that the costumes might be offensive — I had several blind spots like that at the time. The main issue I had was that we were pretending as though we were activists for a cause that neither of us knew anything about, so I felt like a poser. But I didn't have any other ideas, and I was used to doing what other people wanted to do, so I went ahead and wore the costume without much thought.

The day after the party someone left a comment on the social media page for the event about how the organizers should include a disclaimer about the types of costumes that might be inappropriate or offensive, mentioning seeing people wearing headdresses. Those people were J and me. The request was perfectly respectful and well-worded, calling attention to the fact that wearing headdresses as costumes is offensive to many people. J took the comment as an attack and was irate that anyone would challenge her actions, especially given what a great friend she had been to minorities all her life. She immediately went into the thread to defend her reasoning for wearing the costume — claiming that she and I had meant well so there was no justification for being offended, that we were "allowed" to wear headdresses because she had a distant Native American ancestor, and, bizarrely, that I was "part Cherokee." The thread became a back and forth between people trying to explain why they were offended and other people, J among them, explaining why they were wrong to feel offended. The whole situation was making me extremely anxious, but since I didn't understand my emotions at the time, I chose to respond to the anxiety by siding with J, joining in her feelings of persecution. I eventually made a comment on my own, not identifying myself as one of the two who wore the costumes, and saying that "both sides" were being immature.

The story that I wrote about the headdress incident and carried forward for years to come was that I had worn a perfectly respectful costume with a clear, noble message and was misunderstood and publicly attacked. But something about that story didn't sit right and wound up nagging at my subconscious, like so many of the stories that part of me could tell were fabrications. I went on to tell this story to Stephanie in the earlier days of our relationship three separate times in what I now consider a great example of shame venting.

At first, Stephanie gave me the benefit of the doubt, but after hearing the story for the second and third time, she started to wonder why I kept bringing it up, years after the fact. She did a little digging and found an article online about the event, including pictures of J and me in our costumes. At that point she was able to see for herself how ridiculous the costumes actually were. Nobody in their right mind would consider the way we were dressed respectful. We looked like a couple of clowns, doing what could be compared to something like blackface. Stephanie tried to confront me about the photos, but I froze, blamed J for the idea, then went into a shame spiral. She backed off and I buried the experience as best as I could. It came up again a couple months later, though, when she saw the discussion thread on social media, which was in many ways worse than the costumes themselves. She became understandably upset. She wondered how I could find that behavior acceptable — both mine and J's — but I couldn't offer any sort of explanation, as once again, I went into a shame spiral.

What was fortunate about the timing of our second conversation, however, was that it happened right around the time I had started doing daily journaling. This time I didn't bury the subject; I sat with it. I took a good look again at the photos and I read through the comments on social media again. Numerous people offered thoughtful and compelling arguments and posted relevant links that helped me see just how poor my behavior was. I felt an overwhelming amount of shame, but something about sitting with that incident, despite how horrible it made me feel, seemed like the right thing to do. Without fully realizing it, I was trying to process the shame rather than compartmentalize or detach from it. I ended up deleting my old comment on the thread and replacing it with a new one — one that came from the heart, that I wished I had written at the time. I thanked people for having the courage to call out the behavior, apologized for mine, and acknowledged how I've learned from the experience and wouldn't wear a costume like that again. It wasn't much in the grand scheme of things, but it felt as though I had finally properly processed the incident and was able to tell the true story.

Rewriting my stories has often been an extremely painful process. Not only is it destabilizing to challenge the narratives that I have been carrying, sometimes for the majority of my life, but it's also painful to put myself through the experiences again. I am reconnecting to the emotions that I avoided at the time — painful emotions like shame, anger and fear. Early on in the rewriting process, I regularly had moments of doubt and fear that I couldn't handle moving forward, that I wouldn't be able to face yet another confusing incident. Those are the old fears though, the ones that caused me to compartmentalize to begin with. I was able to push through those doubts and allow myself to feel those painful emotions. The more I did so, the more I realized that I could trust myself.

Additionally, the more I revisited my stories, the more I started to see the ways in which it was worth all the pain. Many of the stories that I rewrote wound up actually relieving a tremendous amount of the fear and shame that I had been carrying all my life. Often what I discovered was that the fear and shame had been unfounded — I was not weak or deficient; I did not deserve to be treated badly. I had assumed that other people knew the truth about me. Being honest with myself about when I had been abused was not about playing the victim; it was the opposite. Being abused or mistreated is nothing to be ashamed of and does not need to be hidden from others or from oneself. I am not trying to deny any responsibility and just blame others for what happened. I am attempting to see the full picture, uncover reality and get to the truth.

Perhaps most critically, rewriting the stories of my past brought me closer to understanding who I really was the whole time. I was getting to know myself — the parts of me that I had been hiding from. Gaining an image of the person I *could* have been all those years gave me a map of the type of person I actually wanted to be the whole time. There was no reason that I could see that I couldn't be that person now.

CHAPTER 9: BREAKING THE CODEPENDENCY HABIT

The work I describe in the previous chapters was critical in healing from the trauma that initiated and fueled my codependent behaviors. Understanding the ways in which I was wounded, reconnecting with my emotions, telling the truth to myself and others about my past experiences and present condition, were all important steps. However, the core codependent behaviors — feeling responsible for other people's emotions, compliance, caretaking, people pleasing, compromising my boundaries — were my default ways of interacting with other people since I was a very young child. I needed a new way of relating to people. I needed to see myself as an individual and to understand and value myself. I needed to embrace a new way of being in the world, as an active agent rather than a passive participant.

Getting To Know Myself

Just because I spent most of my life catering to other peoples' wants and needs didn't mean I had none of my own. Just because I avoided expressing strong opinions didn't mean I had no values. Despite the fact that I avoided what my emotions were telling me, my emotions didn't permanently disappear. However blind I kept myself at times, my authentic self was always there, ready to take the stage. In order to act from a place of conscious authenticity, I needed to be sure I understood who I really was all along.

The process of rewriting my stories has involved a significant amount of self-reflection. What emotions was I really feeling at the time? What actions would I have preferred to take in response to those emotions, rather than the action I did take? What did I really feel about the person I was interacting with overall? Was I carrying resentment towards that person? If I were to turn that resentment back into anger, would it have been justified anger, and how would I have preferred to act on that anger? Was I behaving authentically or simply lining up with others? Were there other people affected by my behaviors? Can I empathize with how my behaviors may have made them feel? What can I do to correct the damage?

As I did this forensic work, I not only journalled about what I learned, I built lists that I could refer to as I moved onto another incident, interaction or relationship. In that way, I slowly began to map out my authentic emotional landscape. I would refer back to and keep building on this map as I gained more and more understanding of who I really am and who I want to be.

One of the earliest lists I wrote out was a list of my core values. I listed out what I already respected about myself, the personality traits I found the most valuable, and the types of actions I consider the most important. For me, the list included things like being true to myself, being honest with myself, staying conscious of my empathy for others, and always being curious about myself and others. I find it helpful to have this list handy when reflecting on my past to see when and how I didn't live up to those values. The intention isn't to shame myself. I want a clear picture of where I went wrong, so I can learn from my mistakes and point myself in the right direction moving forward.

This self-reflection work helped me to get in touch with who I am as an individual. Setting aside for the moment what is or isn't within my power to achieve, I want to be sure what my basic needs are, along with my wants and desires and my expectations for the other people. This is not a rigid, unchanging list — my needs and desires are going to be changing all the time. Part of the work is to make sure I prioritize curiosity in myself so that I can recognize and respond to those changes.

Developing Personal Agency

One of the benefits of learning who I really am is that I'm more prepared to move through life with a sense of personal agency. Personal agency refers to the level of control a person feels over their behaviors and actions, and their ability to accept the consequences of those behaviors and actions. A person with a strong sense of agency acts with intentionality. They are committed to taking necessary action to make changes in their lives, rather than letting other people direct what they think or do. Not everything is within one's control, obviously, but someone with personal agency is able to recognize the things that they can or can't control and take action accordingly.

Nobody starts out life with personal agency. There is very little that we have power over when we are very young. A sense of agency typically develops as children move through childhood, adolescence and early adulthood — as they start to make more and more decisions for themselves and build trust in themselves. As discussed in Part 1 of this book, this process was interrupted for me by the trauma I experienced inside and outside my home. Consequently, I spent much of my life without a sense of personal agency. My default position was one of powerlessness.

The more I've learned about myself, the more I've been able to recognize the behaviors that weren't serving me and what was driving those behaviors. I've found it gets easier and easier for me to recognize what power I do or don't have over my environment and when it is or isn't appropriate to take action.

Understanding of my emotions in particular, being able to name them, understand them and react to them in a more informed, intentional, authentic way has been key to building my sense of personal agency. As I began to feel more in control of myself, I began to feel more control of my environment as well. I started to feel as though I could actually make choices, rather than just having to accept whatever came along and make the most of it.

Gaining a sense of agency, like so many other things, has taken some time to start to really sink in. It takes repetition, consistency and lived experience. Recognizing my power and agency has been especially challenging in interpersonal spaces as it involves respecting and defending my own boundaries, something I have always struggled to do.

Boundaries

What exactly does that term boundary mean? It's one of those buzzwords that I heard quite a bit, similar to triggers, and like the word trigger, I struggled to apply it to my own situation. As I tried to figure out my personal boundaries, it helped me to visualize boundaries in their most basic form. Consider a fence between two properties. The fence is there to show where one property ends and another begins. The same applies to people. I am a separate person from you — my body is mine, and yours is yours. That distinction is an example of a boundary. From that straightforward physical example, it becomes more clear how the term applies to other areas of our lives. As my body is mine, so is my time. My emotions are mine. My sexuality is mine. My thoughts and opinions are mine.

Each of us has the responsibility to understand and respect this separation between ourselves and other people. From there, we choose how and when to enforce that separation, depending on the other people involved or the situation. I may choose to share my body, my time, my emotional space, my sexuality or my finances with one or more people, but that is always my choice to make. Yes, there will be times when boundaries are crossed without a person's consent, sometimes violently. The point is to be able to recognize when a boundary is in fact crossed, however it's crossed.

Boundaries and expectations aren't the same thing. Let's say I become involved with someone who smokes cigarettes and I prefer that the person doesn't. I may tell them that a condition for the relationship is that they quit smoking and they agree. But then a week later, I catch them smoking. Then it happens again, and again. I may think "I told this person I didn't want them to smoke, they agreed they wouldn't, and they did it anyway — they crossed my boundary!" Not wanting the person to smoke is an expectation, not a boundary. They didn't cross my boundary, rather they failed to meet an expectation that I had of them. That's not the same thing.

Understanding boundaries involves understanding that not only do you have final authority over yourself, but others have the same authority over themselves. I can have expectations for someone and decide if those expectations aren't met, then I will choose to leave that relationship. But I'd be leaving because of unmet expectations, not because my expectations amounted to a boundary that was crossed. My responsibility is to the boundaries that apply to me, not the other person. It's up to each of us to respect our own boundaries.

I failed to respect my boundaries repeatedly, habitually, in all kinds of interpersonal situations.

People would make requests and demands of me, sometimes respectfully, sometimes not, and I would give in regardless of what I felt about the request or demand. I would often feel resentful that I was being *made* to do things I didn't want to do. Or, like the smoker in the above example, I would sneak around and feel guilt and shame for doing so.

Recognizing and respecting my own boundaries in my existing relationships has been challenging. It takes vulnerability. Doing so has brought to light the nature of a number of those relationships. Some people are respectful when I assert a boundary, such as a desire for space, or a wish to do something different with my time than they would prefer. There are others who respond with guilt, dismissal or even aggression — those are the people I don't want in my life.

As I mentioned earlier, one of the most important things I've done was to look at the various relationships in my life. As I reflected on past relationships, it became clearer and clearer the types of people who did or didn't work for me. But not all of the relationships I reflected on were in the past. How do I see the people who are still in my life — my family, my friends, my current romantic partner, my coworkers? How do I understand those relationships? How do I see myself in those relationships, currently and going forward? Not surprisingly, given the fact I had been behaving codependently for most of my life, I came to find that some of those existing relationships weren't serving me anymore. Some of those people I needed out of my life, and that's okay. I have the right to do that.

Not every person that I choose to keep in my life, however, lines up perfectly with all of my values or expectations. For example, it's certainly possible, but I can't see having a much deeper relationship with anyone from my immediate family. But they're not bad people, and having a relationship with them isn't going to compromise my integrity or threaten my newfound personal agency. Also, I want to continue to have a relationship with them — I choose to. I just need to be sure I understand each of those relationships, what I want from them and what I can offer. I need to have realistic expectations and not feel the need to try to manipulate anyone into being someone they're not, because it somehow makes me feel safer. This is where my boundaries come in. I get to choose how I show up, how I share my time, my thoughts, my space. Actually, my family, as well as my workplace, has been a great place for me to practice recognizing and enforcing boundaries. I've done it pretty regularly now, and have built trust and confidence in myself as a result.

The Codependency Habit

As I've said, I've found that recovering from codependency isn't a matter of identifying unwanted behaviors, then gritting my teeth day after day in an effort to avoid those particular behaviors. People pleasing and caretaking are codependent behaviors, but there's nothing codependent about pleasing people or caring for others. Avoiding my own wants and needs by always prioritizing others' needs is codependent, but that doesn't mean there's never a time or a place to prioritize other peoples' needs. Feeling personal responsibility for other people's painful emotions and trying to defuse them isn't the same thing as empathizing with other people's emotions, being present and feeling a desire to help them. The motivation behind those behaviors matters.

As human beings, we are wired to be responsive to each other. When other people are sad, or scared, or joyous, we feel with them. Whether people react to us with delight, or with anger, or with pride, or with disgust has profound effects throughout our bodies. Let's call this wiring our empathetic system, the various ways in which we are emotionally, mentally and physiologically responsive to others. My empathetic system was hijacked by trauma. Managing my own emotions — my fear, my unease, my shame — was so difficult and overwhelming that I had very little excess capacity. Other people's emotions and behaviors would easily overload my system and feel like threats to me. Rather than feeling with and for people, I was mostly fixated on neutralizing the threats.

Even when I learned about myself and felt more in control of my own emotions, I still felt a need to avoid conflict with other people and to manage other peoples' painful emotions — to behave codependently in other words. Not only were my codependent behaviors habitual, so were the feelings that motivated them. In order to reprogram those behaviors, I needed to get honest about the motivations behind the behaviors and their effects on myself and others.

Take, for example, the codependent behavior of people pleasing. People pleasing can look different depending on the person doing the pleasing. Everyone uses their strengths. For some people, it involves constantly apologizing as a way to disarm any potential conflict, even preemptively. For others it involves excessive complimenting, or extreme rose-colored glasses about anyone and everyone. Another version of people pleasing resembles peacekeeping, where a person feels the need to intervene in other peoples' conflicts in order to smooth things over, make everyone a winner. For me, it mostly involved always trying to tell people what I thought they wanted to hear and trying to be the person I thought they wanted me to be. I worked to make other people feel comfortable, safe and understood at all costs.

People pleasing isn't actually about pleasing people, though. Rather than being based on empathy, it's based on fear — fear of someone being disappointed, displeased, angry, or having some other negative emotional response. People pleasing behaviors have been extremely problematic both for me and for other people in my life. The behaviors kept me stuck in toxic relationships with people who thrived off those types of behaviors. Even in healthy relationships with people I love, my difficulty saying no or asserting my own needs and desires has led to lying and resentment. Rather than attempting to help someone through their painful emotions, I would find myself dismissing those emotions. When it came down to it, those reflexive people pleasing behaviors caused me to choose fear over genuine care, shame-avoidance over intimacy.

Compliance, caretaking, failing to respect my boundaries — these behaviors all had similar motivations for me as people pleasing, and therefore produced similar effects. At the worst, they were, and sometimes still are, reactions to fear. At best, they are simply blind, habitual behaviors. I needed to find a way to be diligent when it came to spotting when I behave in these ways, or better yet, spotting when I feel compelled to. Similar to being on the lookout for when my trauma is triggered, I've looked for all the ways in which my codependent behaviors are activated.

As I explained in the first chapter of the book, codependent behaviors are a solution to powerlessness and the painful emotions that come with it — fear and shame chief among them. Having spent most of my life in a posture of powerlessness, it can be difficult to spot when I'm still feeling that way. I've found that there are a number of clues that alert me to the presence of powerlessness.

One of those clues is when I feel resentment. Resentment is anger stripped of the power to act. I used to feel resentment constantly — against people who I felt were *forcing* me to do things I didn't want to do; against people I didn't even know who had lives and experiences I thought were unavailable to me; against the universe in general for failing to provide me with the things I thought I needed. I've found if I detect resentment at all, however minor, it's almost certain that a sense of powerlessness is present. It's a sign that I'm turning over my power to someone else, then blaming them for *making* me feel powerless.

As with resentment, defensiveness is also often coming from a place of powerlessness. If someone says something that seems to challenge one of my narratives, my system sees that as an attack. In my not-too-distant past, my narratives, however incorrect or unhelpful, were the very weak foundation that held up my whole sense of control. I felt I had no power to act, to make changes in my life, so I could only defend whatever position I already had.

Along with defensiveness or feeling resentful, I find

the impulse to be dishonest, to disguise or dissemble indicates powerlessness. When feeling under threat, lying or at least blurting out the first thing that came to mind was something I did on a regular basis. For instance, I might answer a question too quickly before thinking about it out of fear of being judged for looking unsure of myself.

Watching my language is another way to look for evidence of powerlessness. For example, I find myself overusing the word "we" in places where I should be using "I." Lumping myself together with someone else relieves some of my anxiety and can make it easier for me to shift the blame for any failure to other people. Or when I attempt to express a want or a need, my habit is to express it very passively, ready to shift positions to whatever the other person expressed in order to be sure we were in agreement. These language habits are a sign that I'm reflexively lining myself up with other people, which was one of my core codependent behaviors.

Breaking The Habit

Breaking the habit of powerlessness depended on more than just learning the signs of powerlessness; I also needed to actively make a mental shift from a posture of powerlessness to one of personal agency.

Powerlessness is particularly triggered in me by other people's negative emotions, even minor ones, like disagreement or discord. That sense of powerlessness then activates my codependent response — with resentment, defensiveness and dishonesty often along for the ride. As I discovered when learning how to navigate my trauma triggers, a powerful antidote against this habitual powerlessness response is awareness.

This awareness starts with being conscious of when I feel myself being affected or implicated by another person's negative emotions. What am I actually feeling? I name my emotions and allow myself to feel them. If I sense a trauma response coming on, I acknowledge that and soothe myself however I can in the moment. From that place, it becomes much easier to approach the other person with a calmer, more present curiosity. Rather than going straight to reacting to their emotion, I try to find out why they're expressing it. Do I need to involve myself? Do they even want my help at all? If they do, what can I offer? If I was the cause of the negative emotion, I take a look at my behaviors to see if I agree with their reaction and if there's something I need to do to own up to.

When I introduce awareness into the process of receiving other peoples' emotions, I free up a huge amount of emotional capacity that allows my empathetic system to function properly. When I'm able to be empathetic during someone else's expression of a painful emotion, it allows me the space to approach those expressions with curiosity.

To some extent, this work involves sitting with other people's emotions much as I sit with my own.

In addition to cultivating awareness, I've needed to practice being okay with not only the idea but the reality of disappointing or angering people. This is what being vulnerable, enforcing boundaries, and expressing needs or opinions requires. I've found it helpful to remember that other people are not only separate individuals with their own wants, needs and boundaries, they're also adults who are responsible for their own emotional reactions. As I've learned to trust myself and my ability to stand up for myself, it has given me new insight into what it means for other people to do the same.

I am not trying to completely stop feeling implicated by or responsible for other people's emotions, or to simply mind my own business. Overcorrecting or trying to somehow remove unwanted behaviors isn't the answer, as I might wind up just avoiding empathy altogether. Rather, I am trying to to shift my awareness of what's actually going on and approach interactions with curiosity, rather than with emotionally immature, triggered reactions.

For me healing from codependency has been about learning how to have honest, authentic, connected relationships.

CHAPTER 10:
FINAL THOUGHTS

To some degree, codependency impacted every relationship in my life. Recovering from codependency, re-making my codependent mind, has made it possible for me to rethink, repair and reinvent my social and relational life. I have been able to remove myself from situations and minimize interactions that are damaging to my emotional well being, while leaning in to others with trust and vulnerability in a way that didn't seem possible not that long ago. What has been most impactful by far has been the deepening of my connection with Stephanie and the satisfaction that has brought — loving her and being loved by her has been the miracle of my life.

The road to recovery was not easy. These past few years involved some of the most painful moments I've ever experienced. But the pain felt nothing like the pain of the confusing isolation of my childhood, or the long, lonely years in abusive relationships. There has been meaningfulness in this pain. It was the pain of doing something difficult, something scary that challenged me to grow. With this pain has come a great sense of achievement and satisfaction. I'm proud of what I have accomplished. I'm proud of the relationship Stephanie and I have built together.

That work continues — the work of staying connected to myself and to Stephanie and nurturing our love and commitment. It is the most meaningful work I have ever done and I hope to be doing that work for the rest of my life. What that work is and has been is the topic of the next book.

ABOUT THE PODCAST

This book is based on the podcast of the same name, recorded and released biweekly starting in the summer of 2022. Stephanie and I had been having daily discussions about my codependent behaviors for over a year and those discussions and discoveries were having a huge impact on both of us. We felt that sharing what we had learned could be useful to other people with similar behaviors, while also giving us a way to continue to expand our understanding.

The idea for how we'd approach the podcast took shape right from the start, hence the title we gave it — The Making and the Re-making of a Codependent Mind. The mind in this case is one mind in particular — mine. Rather than attempting to cover every possible way that codependency may start for people or how it may look in broad strokes, we get much more granular with my experiences. Much of the information is presented in a story format, to paint a more complete, vivid picture.

The first two seasons of the podcast cover roughly the same material as this book. If you read the book and go back to the podcast, however, you will notice some key differences. For example, in the podcast, we place more emphasis on the abusive childhood friendship that we describe as being the source of my codependent behaviors, rather than my family, as described in the book. Throughout the course of planning and recording episodes for the podcast, as we had hoped, we learned a lot more about codependency, about my past, about each other and some things became more clear. This book represents my most up to date thoughts.

Subsequent seasons of the podcast expand on various topics as they relate to codependency, like relationships. Even after understanding and healing from codependency, I was still left with re-learning how to navigate relationships in a way that produces the kind of intimate, nurturing connections that I've always longed for. In season 4, we explored what intimacy really is and why codependent behaviors are a block to that. We then explore the various pieces that go into healthy, connected relationships, including what it means to really care for each other. There's so much to cover when it comes to navigating relationships through and beyond codependency that we're working on a second book addressing those topics.

My codependency was about as severe as I can imagine it being for anyone, and the fact that I've managed to navigate my way to the "other side" gives me hope that others can do the same, as long as they're willing to do the work.

ACKNOWLEDGEMENT

To those out there willing to be vulnerable, to face fear and shame in the name of self-knowledge and personal growth, I thank you for what you bring to the world. To our podcast listeners who kept us motivated to dive deeper and continue to expand our understanding of codependency, thank you for your valuable feedback, insight and stories. An extra special thank you to those who came onto the podcast as guests to share their origin stories and messages of hope and recovery. It has given me strength to know I'm not alone in this healing journey. To Ann for your assistance in editing the book, thank you for your honest take and your keen eye. Most of all, thank you to my amazing wife Stephanie, who not only played a vital role in the writing of this book and as a partner in the podcast, but who has helped me along every step of this healing journey. Your empathy, your self-awareness, your vulnerability, your patience, your toughness, your honesty and authenticity, your love. You've opened my eyes to what true connection feels like, what it means to have a real partner in the world.

Made in United States
North Haven, CT
22 November 2024

60737452R00085